No-Talk
Therapy
for
Children
and
Adolescents

By the same author

Violence in the Lives of Adolescents

No-Talk Therapy

for Children and Adolescents

Martha B. Straus, Ph.D.

W. W. Norton & Company
New York • London

For information about permission to reproduce selections
from this book, write to
Permissions, W. W. Norton & Company, Inc., 500 Fifth Avenue,
New York, NY 10110

Composition by Eastern Composition
Manufacturing by Haddon Craftsmen

Library of Congress Cataloging-in-Publication Data

Straus, Martha B., 1956–
    No-talk therapy for children and adolescents / Martha B. Straus.
        p.   cm.
    "A Norton professional book."
    Includes bibliographical references and index.
    ISBN 0-393-70286-3
        1. Child psychotherapy.   2. Adolescent psychotherapy.
    3. Multimodal psychotherapy for children.   4. Play therapy.
    I. Title.
    RJ504.S76   1999
    618.92'8914—dc21   98-44978   CIP

W. W. Norton & Company, Inc., 500 Fifth Avenue, New York, N.Y. 10110
http://www.wwnorton.com

W. W. Norton & Company Ltd., 10 Coptic Street, London WC1A 1PU

1   2   3   4   5   6 7   8   9   0

To my HB, as always,
and to Lizzy and Molly

Time is but the stream I go a-fishing in. I drink at it; but while I drink, I see the sandy bottom and detect how shallow it is. Its thin current slides away, but eternity remains. I would drink deeper, fish in the sky, whose bottom is pebbly with stars.

Henry David Thoreau, *Walden*

Contents

Acknowledgments

I WANT TO THANK MY FAMILY, friends, and colleagues whose support kept me from crawling under the growing piles of laundry and therefore made this book possible.

Thanks to my parents, Betty and Nathan, ever the living proof for me that believing in a kid makes a difference; to my sister Andi who knows that juggling family, work, and life "can't be done" but does it anyway; to my brother Joe, who is actually not as tall as I make him out to be; and to my sensational kids, Lizzy and Molly, who recognize me from the back, typing wildly, all too well now.

Thanks to those gentle readers of the manuscript: John and Julie Kronenberger, Joe Straus, Andi Straus, Tatiana Schreiber, Dan LaFleur, Ph.D., and Cleary Donovan, Psy.D. And especially to Harry Bauld of the green ink, who still wants to know, "How many people *can* be seated in the 'violence arena'?"

Thanks to my dearest friends, Molly and Stacey, who are only far away in miles.

To my editor, Susan Munro, whose unflappability is just what I need.

And especially to the no-talk kids who got me playing again. I would be buried under towels without you.

Preface

WHEN I WAS A KID, RESTLESS and in trouble too much of the time, my father often took me fishing on the Long Island Sound. We'd dig up worms, and row or motor out to a favorite spot near some pilings jutting out of the harbor, throw the anchor over, and sit there, rocking in amiable silence, before going on to another cove, in search of the best action. When we spoke, it was about a nibble, or a decision to switch bait, a snag on the bottom, or the thrill of an occasional flounder on the line. I have no recollection of a conversation of any profound substance or meaning beyond the condition of the old dinghy and the brown water of the Sound. Still, it's obvious to me that we just loved being together. My father didn't know he was the first no-talk therapist in my life.

These fishing excursions came back vividly a few years ago when I was lecturing about depression and self-destructive behavior in kids. Someone in the audience asked, "What do you do when they won't talk to you?" At the time, I improvised some inadequate explanation, realizing that this was a big topic, worthy of more thought than I could supply at the end of a confer-ence. *No-Talk Therapy for Children and Adolescents* is my full answer to that question.

It's a hard time to be a child therapist. At times, I have almost been persuaded by managed care and brief approaches that ther-apy for kids is the same as work with miniature adults. I've apol-ogized to parents when I didn't get their kids "to open up." I've spent fruitless, disappointing hours prying information from re-luctant subjects. I've watched dust grow on my wonderful wooden dollhouse while I set up mind-numbing behavioral con-tracts for miserable seven-year-olds. Too often, I've gotten caught up in the latest techniques, my own agenda for therapy, and generic, impersonal treatment goals. Play therapy almost be-came an indulgence. But really getting to know a kid is not a luxury or a triviality; it is the stuff of good child treatment.

The central point of this book is that sometimes kids don't have to say anything at all to do important work and to feel better. This is a liberating truth for those who are struggling, in vain, to talk about problems with kids. There's a freedom in real-izing it can be therapeutic to spend days shooting hoops with nerfballs and watching teenagers explore their backpacks. For no-talk kids, my office is the dinghy.

More than ever, when kids are brought in for treatment, they feel frightened and helpless. What they need, desperately, is a safe and trustworthy relationship with someone who, in Uri Bronfenbrenner's words, "is crazy about that kid." It isn't always easy to make these connections when kids won't talk. But, as my father taught me, if we can't get the fish to bite in one spot, we can always change the bait, pull up anchor, and try again, over at that fallen tree near the dock.

Here's how.

No-Talk Therapy
for
Children
and
Adolescents

1

Eliza: A No-Talk Kid

ELIZA BENNET IS A FIERCE and wary 15-year-old girl with long dusty dreadlocks, a pierced eyebrow, and an attitude. Following a suicide attempt—a Tylenol overdose—she had been admitted to the mental health unit at the local hospital. Her ten days there had been remarkably disruptive and unproductive. By all accounts, she had turned the place upside down, staging sit-ins at the nurses' station for more cigarette breaks and refusing to attend family meetings. Staff had had to lock the unit after learning she had been organizing an escape for her fellow patients. She would not speak to adults about how she was feeling, but filled notebooks with rageful diatribes about the assault on her dignity there. Eliza had finally signed a discharge contract that included participating in outpatient treatment and taking antidepressants. However, she had added a couple of conditions of her own: She would not "do" family therapy, and she had to regain all the freedoms she had lost before the suicide attempt. With her insurance used up there had been little time for prolonged negotiations.

I agreed to treat Eliza, although I insisted on beginning with the whole family; if Eliza did not want to talk while we discussed other family members' concerns, that would be okay with me. I needed to hear what her parents had to say and wanted to see how she acted with them. Even if I ultimately decided to do mostly individual therapy with Eliza, I still wanted to establish a precedent for parent or family sessions early on, remaining flexible as the work progressed. My first assumption about Eliza was that her terms for therapy—not talking, not wanting her parents present—were a last-ditch effort to preserve self-esteem. She knew that the focus would be on her failures, and she was smart to want to avoid that discussion.

Eliza came with her parents to our first meeting. When I went out to meet her, she was sprawled on a couch in the waiting room looking at a copy of *People* while her parents and other patients were squashed together in the remaining chairs. When I introduced myself, she glanced at me briefly from under piles of hair with piercing hazel eyes. She then returned to her magazine. Eliza's father told her firmly to get up. I offered her a cup of coffee or tea. She poured herself some coffee, dumping six teaspoons of sugar into it while her mother silently grimaced, and sauntered down the hall into my room. Knees tucked under her chin, Eliza glowered at the floor as her parents and I discussed their concerns, the hospitalization, and Eliza's development over the years. True to her promise, she did not speak.

The Bennets shared a litany of disappointment that typically precedes this level of alienation—poor grades, acrimonious family relationships, probable drug involvement, marginal friends, few outside interests. The family had moved from the city to a small town against Eliza's wishes the previous fall, and her adjustment had been poor. While she had once been a helpful oldest sibling, a good student, and a nice kid, she had spent the last year floundering. Her parents had at first been sympathetic to the difficulty of changing schools during sophomore year. Gradually, though, they became less willing to indulge Eliza's griping and began to clamp down on her. Three younger siblings were all doing well. Her suicide attempt followed being grounded for a failing report card. While her parents were upset about the attempt, they also considered it manipulative.

Starting off with all this anger and pain can reinforce a teenager's determination not to talk. In hindsight, it might have been better to have the family meeting later or to hold the first session without Eliza.

I asked Eliza's parents to leave and spent the remainder of the time with her alone. Concerned that she now thought I was "out to get her" like everyone else, I began with the question: "Why do you think I asked your parents for all that information?" She shrugged, and replied, "I have no idea." Like most furious teenagers, Eliza operated under the assumption that adults act *together*, in some sort of conspiracy, in cruel and senseless ways. The past six months of her life had led her to feel she had no say over things that mattered to her; the hospital stay had left her feeling even more powerless, despite her wild protests. Given this recent history, my first priority was to set the record straight: I was different. I had asked the questions because I believed I could help her. I admired her spirit but thought we needed to work a bit on her style. This was *her* therapy and I was not going to take ownership for what happened here. *Together* we needed to come up with a plan. I also said that I hoped we could have fun and that I wanted to get to know her. I gave it my best shot. Then I sat back, telling myself to keep breathing.

After several paleontological eras passed, Eliza sighed, wearily, "It's all so pointless." She stared at the clock and then wedged her coffee cup between two puppets so it looked like they were sharing it.

I saw the prospect for a good existential discussion, but decided that we could do that another time. "That's completely true, and you can still have some fun in the next 70 years," I replied, unwilling to be diverted from a more positive opening. "What do you like doing?"

Eliza looked at me, for perhaps the third time since we had met, and said she wanted to be lead singer in a band someday, even though she knew it wouldn't happen. I wondered out loud why she wasn't starting her own group right now; she had free time and friends who played guitar. Eliza picked at her sneaker and said softly, "Maybe I will." A few minutes later, she walked out without saying goodbye or indicating if she would return the following week.

In no-talk therapy, there is, sometimes, of course, some dialogue, if only now and then. The conversation is seldom, however, about problems and their solutions. When kids don't want to talk, they are typically both bored and degraded by the discussion of their problems. They know the script. Avoiding this, we talk about—and do—things that build kids' sense of competence, comfort in the therapy room, and control over their own behavior. In that first session, my primary aim was to find one thing Eliza enjoyed and felt good about—and to get her to do more of it. I did not ask her about her depression, her family problems, or her hatred of school.

This is not flashy work. Change in no-talk therapy is usually incremental—no "presto change-o" here. It is, more than most therapies, about unseen as well as unspoken connections. A few weeks into the treatment, the relationship feels stronger. Adolescents who have kept tenuous control by remaining mute may be playing five-card stud or sharing a bowl of popcorn. They may even start talking. From the start, kids are involved in finding out about those aspects of their lives they can control and the contributions they can make. With the basis for competence and connection in place, change can follow quite dramatically.

The next week, Eliza brought the copy of *People* into my office with her and asked if she could copy an article in it about a musician she particularly liked. I asked a couple of questions about the music, which she answered briefly and without too much irritation. Encouraged, I asked her to bring in a tape of the group so I could hear it. She did not respond. We then launched into silence. The no-talk dance is a two-step, with the adolescent always leading. In this we are both clumsy; we approach and retreat, not knowing where our feet are all of the time.

A few minutes later, Eliza, glancing around the room, noticed her coffee cup still sitting on the puppet shelf. "Hey, is that mine?"

I was embarrassed at the obvious chaos of my life: "Yes, I suppose it is. I guess I didn't do such a good job cleaning my room."

Eliza seemed delighted, for the first time. "Cool," she said, looking right at me. She gulped down her current drink before placing the second cup inside the first. The seedlings of a relationship began to grow at that moment. We fell silent again, for several minutes, but this time something new was in the air. While I couldn't have planned this intervention, I had the sense to appreciate it. Each week, for the next few months, the stack of cups grew alongside of us.

Part of the early work with teenagers is aimed at making a connection at a safe developmental point—perhaps at a time before life got so difficult. I willingly support regression; if kids don't talk, they still can play. When I pulled out a deck of cards the next week, Eliza looked at me, surprised. I shuffled for a few minutes, engaging her slyly in a conversation about games she liked "as a kid." We played cards in companionable quiet for the next three weeks. She taught me several new card games, patiently going over the rules as necessary. I continued to avoid questions about her life outside the room. However, I did ask each week about suicidal feelings and self-medication with drugs and alcohol; I informed her that I needed to do my job for a few minutes each time we met. Her responses were monosyllabic but reassuring. Even in no-talk therapy, teenagers may be able to tolerate an occasional foray into more typical inquiry, especially if it is brief.

From time to time I also mailed Eliza silly greeting cards to let her know I was thinking about her when she wasn't with me. I have found that this small effort has tremendous significance to teenagers. One of the challenges of no-talk therapy is finding other ways to communicate. Writing notes works on many levels, including the provision of constancy to someone whose world is in flux. I also encouraged Eliza to keep writing in her journal and offered to write her back if she wanted to keep a notebook to share with me. Other no-talk kids have written with me this way. At the very least, my offer told Eliza I was interested in what she had to say. Toward the end of treatment, she did bring in some songs she had written, though she never took me up on my offer to read her other writing.

At the end of the month, Eliza came in and announced that she had signed up, along with four friends, to perform in the high school talent show. She was going to be the lead singer. Clearly excited, she described in great detail what she planned to wear. For a new kid in the school, and one very much on the social fringes, this was a huge and daring step. I was, naturally, very enthusiastic, though it seemed too good to be true. Teenagers who have made such a huge mess of things seldom just snap out of it.

Eliza's mother called a few days later and asked if she could attend a session to discuss the problems Eliza was having at school and at home. She had been caught smoking in the parking lot during class time and suspended. She had stayed all night at a friend's house with several boys, all of them drinking. She had begun hanging around with older kids, some of whom had dropped out of school. While her grades were improving, and she seemed much less depressed, she was still making some bad choices. I agreed that we needed to meet but wanted to strategize with Eliza beforehand to see how to make it helpful to her.

"Your mom called. She wants to come in," I opened the next session. "What do you want me to do?" Eliza was not surprised; her mother had told her this already.

"I'm not coming."

Here we go again, I thought, quickly running through how I felt about all of this. I could simply meet with her mother, but the prospect of discussing Eliza behind her back felt all wrong. If our goal was getting her more in control of her life, she'd have to be a part of this. On the other hand, if I aligned myself with her mother too much, I would lose the fragile connection I had worked so diligently to achieve.

"I want to hear about how you see all of this, but I hope you can also brainstorm with me about how to handle it." I made an effort to get on the same team.

She slowly responded, "I already got grounded for staying out. I don't see the need to talk about this anymore. She wouldn't have let me go if I had told her about it, so of course I lied. What would you have done?" Eliza was mad, but she was telling me about it. I let the silence simmer a minute. Spending the night with drunken drop-out boys, I was thinking to myself. Are you nuts? But I spoke cautiously. We'd been playing a lot of blackjack, so I described what I knew about her gambling style: "You've had a few good hands now. You're feeling better and doing better. People start expecting you to play for higher stakes when you're doing well. But sometimes you gamble way too much and lose most of your savings. You know?" Staying in the playful language enabled us to talk more safely. I let the image sit there, afraid, really, to say more. If I kept at it, we would have entered lecture mode before long. I'd be dishing out gratuitous advice like the clichéd country songs about knowing when to hold 'em and when to fold 'em, and Eliza would probably be entering her no-talk zone.

"I could still get a better hand, you know. You saw me do it." Eliza was in the conversation. We still hadn't resolved anything, but I was determined not to push her any further. Nonchalantly, I grabbed the deck of cards and started shuffling. I was ready if she needed to back off here. She made no gesture toward the poker chips and did not seem to want to play. I kept shuffling. She scowled. Minutes passed. I put down the cards and breathed on.

"So," I finally ventured, "She'll come next time. And. . ."

"I am doing better." Eliza looked tearful; I hadn't seen that face before.

"Okay, that's right. I can tell her that. But how else will you get more chips? If you come, you can say this, too. Otherwise, we'll be deciding it for you." Again, I resisted the urge to solve this for Eliza. We were, briefly, into problem talk, and I didn't want the discussion to replicate her past experiences.

"She treats me like the little kids. It is ridiculous to expect a 15-year-old to be home by 11:00 on the weekend. I'll just stay at Sarah's when I want to go out late; her parents don't care when she comes in." Eliza stared at me, challenging me. I decided to summarize what I thought we were saying. We expect bright and oppositional young adolescents to have abstract reasoning abilities and logical thoughts, but in my experience they seldom do. Refusing to talk, after all, does little for the development of negotiation skills. I saw little percentage in discussing curfews at this point. Eliza lacked the skills and confidence to advocate thoughtfully for herself; it would be an ugly scene. And without a working relationship I was in no position to impart compromising techniques to her. So I kept to a plan that had no new issues, and a straightforward strategy:

"Okay, how about this, then? Your mom will express her concern about the stuff you've been doing. I say I can see why she'd be worried, since I'm a mother, too. It's in our job descriptions, and we're supposed to fret. If you come, you could then say that you have been doing better. I'll completely underscore this. Since I'm such a big fan of yours, this will be easy for me to do. I'm going to ask her to describe some of the changes she's seen. Do you think she's so mad at you she won't be able to do that?"

Eliza shook her head. "She liked my progress reports and she picked me up at rehearsal, so she'd better say that I'm doing more things. And the contract—I'm coming here, and taking my happy pills."

"Money in the bank. Are you ready?" Eliza shrugged. But she seemed to concede she could handle it. I said, "I think you're brave to do this. I know how you feel about family meetings."

The following session went according to our strategy. Mrs. Bennet was able to be enthusiastic about Eliza, after confirming my observations about what had been happening. Eliza knew I was going to be sympathetic to her mother, so she didn't have to worry about my taking her mother's side. While not talkative, Eliza dutifully mumbled out her part about trying harder. I reiterated my sense of her efforts and told Mrs. Bennet she had a great kid. Clearly more worried than angry, Mrs. Bennet even accepted Eliza's proposal to stay at a friend's house that weekend after the grounding ended.

After this, our individual therapy resumed, though not exactly as before. Eliza was more willing to speak to me, particularly after her successful talent-show performance. We still played cards and drew pictures, but these were becoming background activities while we talked. By the ninth session, three months into our work, we were able to begin some of the problem-solving and planning discussions that typify more traditional therapy with adolescents. A family session with both parents was even cheerful. They had visited relatives over spring vacation, and Eliza had been her former helpful self. Along with her confidence, Eliza's grades were improving, and she was staying out of major trouble at home (though admittedly by being smart enough not to get caught). When, a few weeks later (and under pressure from managed care), I suggested we take a break from therapy, she agreed that she was ready. I asked her what I should do with the 12 cups stacked neatly on the shelf. She said, "Keep them here. Put flowers in them." She looked straight at me and smiled.

2

Why Talk Doesn't Work

KIDS DON'T USUALLY WANT to talk about the bad things that have happened to them. For many distressed children and adolescents, participating in therapy is more aversive than cleaning the bathroom. Enraged, sullen, anxious, or confused, they are sent to our offices and endure the hour as squirmy hostages and clock-watchers. They *will not talk* about their feelings; some are even wary of friendly chit-chat.

Any therapist who has ever tried to engage a no-talk kid knows the meaning of frustration and futility. The old standards of "joining"—active listening, supportive reframing, "miracle questions"—provoke only furious silence, toneless monosyllables, hopeless withdrawal, or dripping contempt. For these kids, therapists need an entirely new clinical language that doesn't depend on words. No-talk therapy goes beyond traditional approaches with an emphasis on individual connection, competence, and creativity. It works when we give up on our obsessive need to dwell on problems and find, instead, something to cheer about.

There are times when not talking is the only kind of therapy younger clients can do; they have many potent reasons to remain silent. The seemingly barren therapy hours can cause even the most seasoned clinician to feel like a first-year grad student. And as our anxiety increases, so does the possibility for a frontal struggle in the therapy room. Before we know it, we've become another threatening, cajoling, nagging, and pleading social control agent in a child's life.

By the time they won't talk to therapists, kids usually have had many other people telling them about their ineptitude. They rarely resort to silence as a first defense. As parents, teachers, doctors, and therapists command them to speak, their wordless tenacity merits both empathy and respect. At the same time, they deliver the most difficult and frustrating therapy hours.

No-talk kids can carry a variety of diagnoses. Many start out hesitant about the whole idea of therapy, and a few remain intractably mute despite our best efforts. Some simply aren't ready to talk or play. Others may have an abundance of talking and playing skills but are determined not to use them with us. It is ironic and sad that child therapy, whose most fundamental purpose is to help kids feel better, proves so uncomfortable for so many of them.

Most therapies for kids are too much like simplified versions of adult treatments. Trends in child therapy, spurred by managed care and cognitive-behavioral approaches, are entirely adapted from adult theories. Even the notion that there is something called "child therapy" suggests, erroneously, that there can be treatment for an entire subcategory of people called "children." In fact, it is really only recently that therapists have begun arguing that "children" are a mixed and heterogeneous group, with dramatically varying developmental and behavioral needs (e.g., Kazdin, 1988; Kendall, Lerner, & Craighead, 1984; Shirk & Russell, 1996).

While this more contemporary perspective marks a welcome new era in child therapy, it isn't getting the practical attention it merits. Instead of rigid doctrinaire approaches that fit all children to a given treatment, therapy should be tailored to the needs presented by the particular child or adolescent. This point seems obvious in theory but most therapists are uncomfortable with such a wide-open process. As the saying goes, if all you have is a hammer, you treat everything like a nail.

An individualized, developmental approach encourages us to use a better-stocked toolbox. We should select our tools only after we get to know something about the particular child or adolescent—and not from some preconceived notion of child therapy.

DEVELOPMENTAL RUNWAYS

In work with no-talk kids, chronological age is seldom very informative. Consider the many different kinds of "runways" children must go down en route to adulthood: physical, cognitive, emotional, and social. Children "take off" at different speeds along a unique combination of developmental trajectories. For example, some kids who are very bright and cognitively advanced are also very immature and emotionally delayed. Some who are physically mature are socially awkward. Some kids have enormous discrepancies in development, while others seem more all-of-a-piece. By the time they arrive mutely in a therapist's office, though, it is highly likely that no-talk kids are stuck somewhere along the way, and they *will* be functioning at a younger age in one or more spheres.

Although take-off is possible on many kinds of runways, therapists still need to keep in mind the "normal range" in child development. When we compare kids referred for therapy with peers who are generally managing their lives more skillfully, we catch a glimpse behind the curtain of silence. Therapists tend to develop a skewed perspective on child development; we sometimes forget that the majority of kids out there have dry beds and unpierced navels. Comparative developmental information casts light on the particular strengths and difficulties the child or adolescent might have; it helps us maintain a more dynamic understanding of how she is functioning at a particular moment and, at the same time, keep track of where she is headed. Even more importantly, consideration of these various "runways" suggests how complex and difficult therapy can be for angry, traumatized, and overwhelmed kids. Extending the runway metaphor, not enough fuel, too much baggage, confusing instrumentation, and terrorists on board can all impede successful take-off.

Physical Development

Psychotherapists pay insufficient attention to the dramatic physical changes that kids undergo from year to year. We're mostly interested in what's happening above the neck. Yet, physical maturation is a big deal for *all children*. When we ignore what it's like to be transforming in shape and size so rapidly, we only emphasize our tacit belief that kids are just vertically-challenged adults. The connection between the work of psychotherapy and physical development is worth some contemplation: How old does the child or adolescent appear to be? For which developmental milestones has he been late, and why? Are the expectations of others (parents, teachers, therapists, peers) physically attainable? Since self-esteem depends so much on this, how *do* kids feel about their appearances? The physical maturity of children, their physical gifts or disabilities, the discrepancy between how old they are and seem, their attractiveness in the eyes of others, and their developmental history all have an impact on the quality of the therapeutic relationship.

Puberty is probably the most confusing aspect of physical development for therapists (as it is for many people). That developmental interlude once called "latency" doesn't exist much anymore—if it ever did—and the "preadolescent" is often a child as young as eight or nine. For example, Amy, a nine-year-old was referred because she seemed to have mood-swings. She would giggle hysterically or collapse into a sobbing pile for seemingly trivial reasons. Her parents also noted that she flew into rages, accompanied by door slamming and stomping around in her room. Amy was entering puberty, with a little acne on her nose, a voracious appetite, and developing secondary sex characteristics. If she had been 14 years old, her parents probably wouldn't have found anything surprising in her behavior.

The emotional fluctuation once associated with "normal" teenage hormones describes many younger kids, too. More than one parent of a difficult girl has wondered bemusedly just how long PMS can last. Kids who physically mature early are sometimes capable of a remarkable range of behavior; they are held back by limited experience and social immaturity on one end, and driven by biochemistry and *pseudo*maturity on the other. The mass-media culture also promotes a facade of physical maturity in young children by blurring distinctions between fashion and entertainment—six-year-olds wear the same kinds of jeans and sneakers that 16-year-olds do, play the same computer games, and eat the same junk food. Careful not to infantilize our younger clients, we tend to err instead in the direction of expecting too much, basing our information on how old they *appear* to be—or wish they were.

But if puberty poses problems, so does a lack of physical maturity. Kids who are later than average in developing have their own share of unhappiness. They tend to lack self-confidence and are often relatively anxious and tense compared to their more developed age peers (Fenwick & Smith, 1996). The impact of physical development upon psychological functioning merits close attention as individual treatment planning proceeds. Comparing themselves to adults, kids often feel even smaller and younger than they appear. But, as in all areas of child development, the range of possibilities is wide.

Cognitive Development

Cognitive development is another long runway toward adulthood. Many kids who have trouble discussing their problems in treatment simply lack the cognitive skills that are the basis for talking therapies. These children and adolescents aren't able to think about or describe their difficulties in a useful way. In Piagetian terms, they may not be fully in "concrete operations," though they are well over the age of seven, or in "formal operations," though they are teenagers (Piaget, 1954).

While children are maturing physically at younger ages than in the past, there is ample evidence that their cognitive development is actually less rapid, particularly for kids with other kinds of problems (e.g., Guerra, 1993 Healy, 1990). The implications of this for therapy are significant. No-talk adolescents rarely use formal operational thought; some have only early concrete operational strategies. They live, egocentrically, in the present and struggle to anticipate any consequences they have not experienced *repeatedly*. For example, one 16-year-old boy needed to be punished by each of his teachers for skipping class before he improved his attendance. Similarly, the cognitive range for younger kids is also considerable. Many children who are well over seven are still largely preoperational in the way they approach the world—with little ability to think things through in more than one rather obvious way.

Because they tend to reason like younger children, no-talk kids pose a challenge for traditional therapy, even if they do start talking. Many children and adolescents develop more mature problem-solving strategies in the course of time, but at the outset of therapy they may well be thinking like someone significantly younger. Notably, not talking about problems tends to compound cognitive delays. To develop alternative strategies for managing their lives, these kids need lots of opportunities to plan, problem solve, think before reacting, make predictions, and wonder.

Language development is, of course, the window into much of the problem-solving that goes on in a therapist's office. When kids won't say much, we shouldn't assume they have the language skills to handle the kinds of therapeutic discussions we want to have. It is surprising how little knowledge most therapists have about the variety of language delays that kids can have. The course or two in psycholinguistics we might have taken along the way rarely informs how we work.

An ability to understand and use increasingly complex and abstract language is closely tied to the development of cognitive and social skills. Before age 10, for example, many kids are quite concrete and contextually-bound in their use of language. Only some no-talk kids can understand metaphor or abstract concepts. They can, increasingly, talk about a range of experiences (though not so much about how they are feeling) and also, by early adolescence, engage in more active verbal problem-solving. For example, they can brainstorm to create a list of possible outcomes for staying out past curfew. But these verbal skills evolve gradually, from the here and now to a consideration of what might happen at other times and places.

The language of therapy is also complex for some kids because it involves comprehension of the unusual way we want to enter into a relationship with them. Kids may not understand the personal questions we are asking—or why we are asking them. They may have difficulty following the "drift" of our inquiry, and they may not be able to ask for clarification when they feel clueless. Even kids who express themselves relatively well may shrug mutely when we begin, "How can I be helpful to you?" or "What did your mother tell you about why she wanted us to meet?" There are many places that kids can get lost following a conversation, starting with our kind first words. For therapists, then, using simple vocabulary and sentences is only part of the job. We want so much for kids to talk with us that we sometimes overlook the possibility that they don't really know how.

Emotional Development

Therapy aims to help children and adolescents identify and make sense of their internal states. A growing body of research suggests that the *experience, expression,* and *regulation* of emotions follow a predictable developmental timeline (for a detailed review of these data, see Shirk & Russell, 1996). No-talk kids are struggling with their inner worlds and invariably show significant delays in emotional development.

Emotional Experience

Therapists often place high value on helping children identify their feelings and describe them with words—an emphasis derived directly from the treatment of adults. The capacity to attend to, understand, and talk about emotions is, of course, the essential focus of adult psychotherapy (e.g., Greenberg & Safran, 1987). In adult treatment, successful outcomes appear to be linked to this ability to focus on and understand emotional experience. But for kids such skills may develop slowly, if at all. This fact alone is sufficient to distinguish child from adult therapy.

Emotional experience is made up of a complex network of interrelated abilities, each with its own developmental course. The first task is the recognition and identification of feelings. As they get older, kids become increasingly capable of sorting out subtle differences in emotions. This ability, in turn, is closely connected to the development of a more sophisticated and nuanced vocabulary that can be applied to the feelings. Older children's emotional inferences also become more subtle, and they move away from the simple labels—glad, sad, mad, bad, scared—to more specific emotions like proud, ashamed, grateful, bewildered, and relieved. But the process is more difficult than merely labeling emotions; it also entails an ability to grasp the meaning of emotional experiences. For example, a child who becomes easily upset and understands that she is exhausted has a different explanation for her irritability than one who becomes similarly upset but believes she feels this way because her parents are being unfair.

When kids don't talk in therapy, they may not recognize their feelings, they may not be able to put them into words, and they may not be able to understand the meaning of these emotions. But their emotional experience is even *more* complicated because these kids typically have endured hard times that produce many concurrent and conflicting feelings. Abused kids provide a clear example of this; they may feel love, fear, rage and sadness, among other potent emotions—often all at once. Research in emotions suggests that, in general, mixed emotions are impossible for most five-year-olds to describe; description remains difficult for six- and seven-year-olds, and only becomes increasingly possible for eight- to ten-year-olds. Seven-year-olds can be aware of two emotions at the same time if they do not appear incompatible and are directed toward the same event. They can understand how they might be both happy and excited about getting a present. Not until around ten years can most children comprehend that they can have two incompatible emotions— and even then only if the two emotions are evoked by two different situations. They can be thrilled about taking an airplane and scared about being away from home for a long time. It really requires the onset of formal operations—12 years or more—before most children understand that contradictory emotions can be directed toward the same event. They can be upset that the coach yelled but glad he was honest (Brems, 1993; Harter & Whitesell, 1989. These developmental levels have immediate and vital links to the practice of therapy, highlighting the unrealistic expectations many of us may have when we ask about the emotional experiences of our younger clients. When children seem unable to describe their emotional states, we must be alert to the many reasons why this is so difficult for them.

Emotional Expression
Children may enter therapy because their expression of emotions worries adults. Whether they are acting out distressed feelings or concealing them, something seems awry in the communication. These kids may not express themselves verbally because they are unwilling or unable to talk about emotional experience. Children of all ages vary widely in their tendency to avoid emotionally charged discussions, but most of the research

to date indicates that this, too, has a strong developmental component (e.g., Smith & Rossman, 1986).

For example, children under seven are more likely to deny and distance themselves from negative feelings like sadness and to present uniformly happy self-portraits; older kids between seven and 11 tend to project negative feelings onto others while they deny their own. Generally, young children tend to be more adept at labeling emotions and hypothesizing about feelings when the emotions in question are not their own. For example, even kids under seven can explain why a puppet is crying and think about what might make it feel better. If they have sufficient language skills, they will also be able to figure out a response to a speculative question like, "How will the puppet feel if _____?" Thus, a child's expression of feelings may be greater when her own pain or confusion isn't the central concern.

The research literature on the development of emotional expression concludes consistently: *It is relatively rare for a preadolescent child to be a willing participant in a discussion of negative feelings.* Many adolescents are similarly reticent. An evolving ability to put miserable events into feeling words explains, in part, why *most* kids have trouble talking directly about intense experiences while they are in therapy. This is why the indirect and symbolic backdoor approach of play therapy is frequently more effective than conversation with younger kids.

Emotional expression in therapy is also a problem because kids live so much in the present, when we want them to talk about how earlier experiences made them feel. They may understand emotions in a given situation and emotions linked to specific behaviors (e.g., hitting when angry or crying when sad), but we want them to dig into the past and dredge up a mine of unexpressed emotion that has been buried under the passage of time. We may think they are resisting telling us "how they felt," but it is also possible that they have not yet acquired the developmental ability to recognize and appreciate the enduring nature of feelings. Children under seven have particular difficulty coordinating feelings evoked by immediate situations with feelings related to prior experiences (Donald & Westerman, 1986). While they sit anxiously in our offices, it's hard for many kids to describe even yesterday's emotions.

With older children and even some adolescents (particularly no-talk kids), the quest for emotional expression in therapy can lead to similar bewilderment and lack of interest. Most of us have had our probing question, "How did you feel when that happened?" swatted away with a terse "Fine" or "I don't know." This can reflect developmental immaturity even in children older than seven. When kids come from homes where "talking about feelings" isn't the norm, this line of inquiry may seem as confusing as driving in Boston for the first time. For some children and adolescents, the possibility of an emotional meltdown—becoming so overwhelmed by raw feeling that they can't make sense of it—is also great. And then they won't be able to think coherently about feelings anyway, as anyone who has sat with a raging or sobbing child knows.

We shouldn't jump to the conclusion that kids are being defensive when we try to talk about past feelings. Their tendency to distance themselves from strong negative feelings is developmentally typical for preadolescents, and fairly common for teenagers as well. At the same time, if the aroused emotion is too strong, children can't begin to make sense of it in any beneficial therapeutic way, and it may even make therapy more aversive. In our work with children, we must first be certain that they share our capacity for a thoughtful review of old emotions—or else find other ways to help them express themselves.

Emotional Regulation
Children often enter therapy because they can't regulate their emotional world. They have temper tantrums, cry when someone looks at them "the wrong way," or get into fights at the slightest provocation. Most disorders of childhood seem to involve some kind of problem with emotional regulation (Cole,

Michel, & O'Donnell, 1994; Shirk & Russell, 1996), so it is note-worthy that this aspect of emotional development also requires its own runway.

Over the years, children become increasingly competent at both modulating their emotional experience (beyond the all-or-none method of preschool emoting) and controlling the expression of feeling by restraining themselves and using words instead of actions. The infant and young child rely to a great extent upon the support of adults to help them regulate their emotions; strong attachments are the cornerstone of this developing capacity. The upset toddler relies on a caring adult to kiss his bumps and bruises and to hold or remove him from the scene when he loses control.

As children get older, they're expected to take on the tasks of calming and regulating themselves. For example, most school-age children are capable of feeling very angry without becoming violent. Emotionally attached kids additionally develop a kind of "dimmer switch" that enables them to react in proportion to the intensity of experiences. They have benefited from consistent adult responses to all their different feelings; someone has been there to interpret the emotional world for them. School-aged kids should show signs of emotional regulation; we assume that they'll become angrier when someone intentionally hits them than when someone accidently bumps into them, that they'll cry more when they're hurt more, that they'll calm down within a reasonable amount of time.

By adolescence, though, problems with emotional regulation are compounded by hormones, increased external expectations for emotional control, and dramatically decreased adult interven-tion. Thus I often am referred young adolescents with problems in emotional regulation that appear to be of relatively recent onset. In therapy, these kids seem to have only two modes of operating: out of control or shut down. Particularly if they have a history of early losses, they'll need to learn how to modulate feelings—maybe for the first time. When kids have a troubled attachment history, it's likely that they will be quite infantile in their ability to regulate their emotions. They'll need to develop both better defenses and better skills.

Social Development

Therapy is essentially a social activity. Even play therapy, which permits a child to retreat into a more isolated fantasy world from time to time, has at its foundation a developing, purposeful relationship. Since kids come into therapy with a lifetime of other social experiences, their expectations for this relationship will have roots in their social history. And no-talk kids evidently don't expect much.

Like all of us, no-talk kids draw "social maps"—they place themselves in their worlds informed by the influences of development, temperament, family, school, neighborhood, community, and culture. As Garbarino (1995) aptly notes:

> Some children learn to draw social maps in which they are central figures, powerful and surrounded by allies. Others draw defensive maps in which they are surrounded by enemies, or are insignificant specks, stuck off in the corner. Does the child expect help when in need? Does the child fear strangers? Does the child trust other children? Does the child expect adults to cause pain? To give comfort? Does the child see a safe and secure place in the world? The social map holds the answer to these questions. (pp. 23–24)

No-talk kids may draw social maps that evolve into unfortunate self-fulfilling prophesies. Over time, they both react to and create their social worlds. Expecting to be hurt as they have in the past, they act preemptively, ensuring the very rejection and abandonment they fear the most. Their social maps help explain how they have come to have so much trouble making a connection with us.

As a rule, social development has not progressed smoothly for kids who won't talk in therapy. They are often quite disengaged, at least from the conventional ways of interacting. If they have some friendships, these may be with other similarly alienated and hurting kids, on the community margins. Their lack of social success outside of the therapy room bodes poorly for them, and for the therapeutic relationship. Therapy can make a difference if it leads them to greater social competence and confidence. But it is usually evident from the outset that these kids are drawing very defensive social maps; they lack the social skills they so urgently need to develop.

From a developmental perspective, as children move from egocentrism to more capable perspective-taking, their relationships deepen and vary. Forming and maintaining a satisfying social life is a central developmental task. Children and adolescents who have close friendships and are accepted by peers typically are high in self-esteem, socially skilled, and academically successful (Berndt & Savin-Williams, 1993). As a corollary, children and adolescents who lack supportive friendships or who are rejected by many of their peers show poor psychological, social, and academic adjustment (Parker & Asher, 1987). Longitudinal studies have even demonstrated a significant relationship between how well children and adolescents get along with their peers and how well adjusted they are as adults (e.g., Dodge, 1989).

In addition, socially successful kids usually have mostly enjoyable relationships with parents and other adults. Their confidence crosses generations. And, even though adolescent conflict with adults is inevitable as they wend their way toward separation, these teens still maintain a vital connection to family and the grown-up world. In all ways, getting down the social runway is essential for a well-adjusted life.

The Runway Problems of Traumatized Kids

Many kids who are sent to therapy have lives that are unspeakably hard. These traumatized children and adolescents have "runway problems" that make traditional therapy impossible. They've become no-talk kids through enduring traumatic events that are too painful to talk about. Violence and fear affect all kinds of development by both delaying *and* distorting it.

The effect of trauma on physical development, especially on neurochemistry and physiology, is well documented. Usually traumatized no-talk kids have significant deficits in physiological regulation. They may suffer from hyperarousal, hypervigilance, anxiety, panic, startle responses, tremors, numbing, and the full range of post-traumatic stress symptoms. These kids are often working full-time just to manage their physiological reactivity. Therapy for kids in this kind of physical state helps them learn to relax, self-soothe, and know when they are becoming physiologically aroused.

No-talk kids also often have an assortment of cognitive deficits. Trauma, abuse, neglect, and disruptions in attachment can all throw Piaget's timeline into complete disarray. Typical cognitive problems include visual or auditory processing difficulties, thought inflexibility, delays in verbal skills, poor social reasoning, and other types of learning and attention difficulties.

The harmful effects of violence on emotional development are also important to note. They include, for example, the traumagenic states described so sensitively by Beverly James (1989): dissociation, depersonalization, self-blame, betrayal, erotization, helplessness, anxiety, depression, panic, rage, detachment, and destructiveness. Violence, shattering basic trust, can make it nearly impossible for these kids to get down the emotional runway. They typically veer off the path in many places along the way.

When no-talk kids are coping with trauma in their lives, they will also invariably be evincing particular kinds of significant social problems. These may include, for example, appearing clingy or detached, lacking emotional reciprocity and empathy, exhibiting overcontrolling relationships with peers, disregarding personal space, acting aggressively, engaging in dissociated social and sexual encounters, displaying a tenacious investment in sabotaging social possibilities, and maintaining traumatized attachments. As therapists, we have to meet them at their developmental level. A traumatized 12-year-old can actually have more in common, socially, with the toddler set. Thus, therapy needs to focus on strengthening positive attachments, teaching social problem-solving skills, increasing social and sexual safety, and establishing fundamental therapeutic trust as a basis for other relationships.

The connection between trauma and difficulty talking in therapy has been clearly established. Kids who have been victimized and exposed to violence have many compounding reasons that make therapy frightening and hazardous for them. Developmental deficits and fundamental mistrust lead logically to the no-talk zone. When we are beginning to treat a traumatized no-talk kid, we have additional obstacles to overcome.

SUCCESSFUL INTERVENTIONS

No-talk kids fit so many descriptions and can be reached in such a variety of ways that it may be unnecessarily reductionist to try to describe what makes interventions work. It is likely, however, that five broad principles are operating when no-talk therapy succeeds:

1. No-talk kids have the opportunity to develop healing relationships with trustworthy adults in a place they perceive to be safe.

2. Other services are also provided (e.g., family therapy, tutoring, social skills groups, job placement, trumpet lessons), because no-talk kids are complex and require individualized, multisystemic supports.

3. The peer group is recognized as a powerful source of support and connection, and efforts are made to develop social skills among peers.

4. Therapy meets the child or adolescent at an accurate developmental point on the runway. Physical, social, cognitive, or emotional delays are addressed through building competencies and skills.

5. Family members are involved in treatment to the extent that they are willing and able. The circle of adults embraces all of the people who care about the child *and* other family members. Our work always points kids in the direction of being more successful in their families and communities.

These basic principles can be hard to put into practice with no-talk kids; our erroneous assumptions about child treatment get in the way.

THERAPIST ASSUMPTIONS

Good therapists are prepared to identify and accept children at their particular developmental levels, use language suitable to the task, tolerate regression as it inevitably surfaces, and involve family, school, peers, and community in the therapeutic process. But even so, some kids are distinctly unappreciative of this thoughtful benevolence and offer nothing in return. Why?

Even though we may be well-intentioned, therapists generally operate under five child-unfriendly assumptions derived, incorrectly, from our treatment of adults: (1) Talking is the most natural way of exchanging information; (2) talking about problems leads to solutions; (3) getting in touch with bad feelings is beneficial; (4) talking in therapy leads people to have more control over their lives; and (5) the prospect of feeling better through talking is inherently motivating. While even very articulate, sensitive kids would probably disagree with these premises, it doesn't take any words at all for a child to demonstrate how inadequate these assumptions are.

Talking to Adults Is Not Natural for Kids

Talk, for adults, is a method of communication honed over the years. Even so, most of us are pretty tongue-tied when we're describing how we feel. Kids rely less on talking and more on other sources for information about the world and their place in it: what others are doing, tone of voice, body language, expectations, past experience, degree of fun, and consequences.

In fact, therapy's typically exclusive reliance on dialogue sets it apart from all the other relationships that children commonly have. For example, in school, children may be called upon to respond to isolated requests for information or to offer ideas of their own, but they are seldom held in a sustained one-on-one conversation with an adult. Moreover, most of the research on communication with parents at home indicates that American mothers spend less than half an hour a day talking or reading with their children or explaining things to them; fathers spend less than 15 minutes a day (Institute for Social Research, 1986; United States Department of Education, 1987). Even when children or teenagers get together, they may be talking, but they are also usually doing something else—playing games, competing in sports, listening to music, making things, hanging out. Consequently, a prolonged conversation with anyone, much less an unfamiliar adult, is a bizarre idea for most kids—a most unnatural way of exchanging information. Even more willing participants can find therapy daunting.

This problem may be more of a two-way street than we'd like to think. It's fairly hard for most of *us* to keep kids engaged in dialogue for an hour at a stretch. Interestingly, it's no easier in family therapy than in individual therapy to talk with kids, especially younger ones. Family therapists often direct their comments to parents while the child or adolescent listens (or doesn't). Younger clients, in particular, tend to sit and play while the adults in the room talk and argue about them. In fact, about 85 percent of therapist comments in family sessions with young kids are directed toward parents (Cederborg, 1997). Even if we set aside all of the critical variables imaginable—developmental level, cultural emphasis on language, social skills, who is present, motivation, degree of distress, and even the time of day—many kids are *still* relatively unprepared to spend fifty minutes just jabbering with a grown-up.

Talking about Problems Makes Problems Bigger

Another dearly held assumption that guides most therapy is the notion that to solve problems we must first talk about them. For many adults who seek out therapy this is the primary focus. We may talk about our depression by describing in considerable detail the neglectful parenting we received, or about our stress at work by outlining the unreasonable demands of our employer. Even the solution-focused therapies first begin with some close attention to the story of the problem. Adults love (or at least accept) these strategies and usually find them very useful. But this is a much more arduous task for most children and teenagers; kids who don't talk about problems are letting us know, in no uncertain terms, that this approach will not work.

There is also some evidence, even in the adult literature, that talking about problems can often intensify them. Indeed, people who focus exclusively on their depression usually feel similarly depressed at the end of the hour. People with anxiety can become *more* anxious thinking about it. It makes good sense that most of the current approaches for treating both anxiety and depression in adults focus more on building on exceptions and competencies. Of course, some of us like to rant a bit to get things off our chest, and there are even kids who come in and let words fly and then feel better. But these conversations are about transient kinds of problems, experienced by people who know how to bounce back, and not the deeper and more intractable struggles people have. It is safe to say that no-talk kids aren't this resilient.

For many kids, the distinction between having problems and being bad is often blurred. Even when concerned adults encourage the belief that "You're a good person who does bad things," most kids, especially those who have made a really big mess, don't believe it. Discussion of problems for them is redundant and cruelly overwhelming. Under the guise of helpful criticism (an oxymoron if there ever was one), adults who launch into a recitation of all that has gone wrong are perceived as *un*helpful. It is better to follow that old Jackson Browne song line, "Don't confront me with my failures, I've not forgotten them." Kids who don't talk to therapists *know* they are the problem, so it will only underscore their certainty to focus on it.

Getting in Touch with Bad Feelings Makes Kids Miserable

Another of the goals of adult treatment that doesn't translate to kids is the whole fascination we have with talking about feelings, especially lousy—mad, sad, bad—feelings. Our insistence on dwelling on all that emotional content makes therapy both frightening and annoying for many children and adolescents. For adults, being vulnerable and open in therapy is generally cathartic; for kids it can feel like a complete rending of whatever fragile protective shield they may have. Not talking under these circumstances, when no other defenses are available, makes perfect sense. It takes the development of a very trusting relationship to enable troubled kids, even if they are highly verbal, to feel safe enough to describe their wretched internal states. And, of course, this presupposes that they *can* put internal experience into words—a task that even most adults find difficult.

Yet therapy typically begins with precisely this emphasis. Our concern may be genuine when we offer our sympathetic comments. But even a statement as simple as, "It sounds like you're having a tough time," is filtered through the no-talk lens. It has been my experience that these kids take such comments as further indication that we intend to conduct an all-out assault on their dignity and their very ability to get through the day. In some ways, they are all too connected to their horrible feelings; asking them to dwell in these depths is a hellish and cruel endeavor.

Therapy Talk Doesn't Give Kids More Control over Their Lives

Children and adolescents don't have control over their lives. Adults can decide to move, change jobs, divorce, refuse medication, ignore their parents, sleep all day, eat Oreos for breakfast, and purchase unnecessary electronic devices. But for the most part, kids have astoundingly fewer options as to what will happen to them. They are, in essence, stuck with the reality of their schools, families, neighborhoods, allowance, and menu—a fact that points child therapy in a dramatically different direction from the course of adult treatment. A compelling example of this powerlessness can be seen in the area of child abuse, where, even if children are removed from abusive homes, a reunification plan is quickly enacted. By contrast, we would not dream of telling a battered wife she had to leave *or* return to her batterer. Adults make the decisions for kids. Therapy for children and adolescents has to focus more on helping them adapt to and manage the reality of their lives than on how they can change it.

The same notion of control is critical in the therapeutic relationship as well. In many ways, traditional talk therapies mirror real life experience by adhering to adult rules and expectations for behavior. Everywhere kids go, grown-ups have agendas. At home, they're supposed to clean their rooms and eat vegetables; at school they have to raise their hand before they speak and complete assignments according to teacher preferences; and in therapy they need to sit for 50 minutes and talk about what is bothering them. For the therapeutic relationship to be different, then, we need to attend to this notion of control. Most kids do not enter therapy willingly or view it as their idea. Many don't even know what therapy *is*. Giving children a share in the process and outcome can be a real challenge, but it can distinguish therapy from other parts of their lives in important ways.

Change Isn't Inherently Motivating to Kids

Adults often seek out therapy with the idea that making changes in their lives would be a good thing. Similarly, parents and other people who help children and adolescents get into treatment have hopes that these kids will act, feel, or think differently afterwards. Adults believe that the rewards to come from "getting better" are sufficient to motivate the struggles along the way—for everyone. But, from a purely developmental angle, there is really no way children—and most adolescents—can comprehend this point. As with getting shots, the notion that, down the road, the pain will be worth it, is of little practical value for most kids, who live largely in the present moment.

Even if the abstraction of feeling better made sense, kids are inherently conservative creatures, viewing change as undesirable. It is likely that they enter therapy for extrinsic reasons (pleasing parents, avoiding punishment) and not out of a desire to change their lives.

In fact, no-talk kids seldom believe they "need" therapy. And, even if they agree to it, they may have a definition of the problem that doesn't match their parents' description. For example, a child whose behavior leads to fights at home may believe that the conflict is precipitated by his parent's unreasonable requests—that his own defiance is merely a necessary response. In this case, the problem that needs to be fixed may lie in the parent's behavior; if so, it might be possible for the child to remain silent—without doing much differently at all.

SPEAK NO EVIL

We are often asked to heal the effects of violence against kids; we must also acknowledge the assault upon childhood itself. Developmental runways and our faulty assumptions still describe only part of the no-talk story. The rest might be explained by the interaction between the child and his environment—the family, culture, and community. The social maps that these kids draw portray environments that have been traumatizing and unsupportive. Even the most resilient child or adolescent with the finest genetic endowments would have a stressful time with these stories, in these families, on these streets, with so few resources aimed in his direction. In runway terms, these kids have a harder time "taking off" because they are on swampy land. (It's also tougher for their therapists to get to the "plane" to find out why it's still on the ground.) The reality is that, for kids with developmental problems or delays, the compounding effects of a harsh environment can make putting experience into words nearly impossible.

Most therapists who have worked with kids over several decades agree that their problems are more severe today than in the past. These observations have been supported by research and in a range of national reports and clinical studies (e.g., Achenbach & Howell, 1993; Dryfoos, 1990; Garbarino, 1995; Healy, 1990; Hewlett, 1991; Pipher, 1994; Select Committee on Children, Youth and Families, 1989; Straus, 1994). The overwhelming sense that these findings convey is that our job is getting harder. Even kids in the general population have more problems and greater severity of distress (Achenbach & Howell, 1993).

These difficulties in coping are obviously compounded by the fact the environment is becoming increasingly hostile to children and teenagers Garbarino, 1995; Males, 1996; Select Committee on Children, Youth and Families, 1989). Though no-talk kids come from all types of situations, most have endured what Garbarino (1995) calls a "socially toxic environment"—the social world in which they live has actually been poisonous to their development. The following are just a few compelling examples.

Gun Violence

Suicide by guns has increased 132 percent in the past 50 years. Guns in the home are used for suicide 40 times more often than for self-protection. In fact, two-thirds of completed suicides by adolescents are gun deaths. Similarly, the firearm homicide rate for 10- to 14-year-olds more than doubled between 1985 and 1992. In one survey, 39 percent of children in grades 6 to 12 knew someone who had been killed or wounded by gunfire, and nearly 60 percent said they could get a gun if they wanted to. Compared with children in 25 other industrialized countries combined, U.S. children under age 15 are 12 times more likely to die from gunfire, 16 times more likely to be murdered by a gun, 11 times more likely to commit suicide with a gun, and nine times more likely to die in a firearm accident. Not surprisingly, the greatest worry of 10- to 17-year-olds is violent crime (American Psychological Association, 1996; Children's Defense Fund, 1998; Garbarino, 1995).

Media Violence

By sixth grade children have witnessed 8,000 television murders and 100,000 other acts of television violence, and these numbers don't include video games, movies, and other media. The American Psychological Association (1993) concludes that television is responsible for over 15 percent of the violent behavior of kids. Television and video games have also replaced activities that might otherwise be shared with family and friends. The substitution of passive observation for real social interaction diminishes opportunities for social learning and appears to increase distrust. In addition, kids feel less safe and draw more fearful social maps.

Childhood Trauma

Dryfoos (1990) states that seven million adolescents—one in four—are at severe risk for encountering serious problems at home, in school, and in their communities, These kids tend to be functionally illiterate, disconnected from school, depressed, and prone to drug abuse; they are likely to engage in early criminal activity and eventually to become parents of unplanned and unwanted babies.

While there are no national reports, estimates of children who have post-traumatic stress disorder (PTSD) symptoms are quite high in specific areas. For example, as many as 40 percent of children in violence-ridden neighborhoods may be trau-matized, and as many as 60 percent had PTSD after a school-yard sniper attack (Amaya-Jackson & March, 1995). We can only imagine the lasting psychological effects on the one in four 10-to 16-year-olds in a national survey who reported being assaulted in the previous year. Similarly, we can expect enduring emo-tional trauma for the one in three girls and one in five boys who are sexually abused by the time they turn 18 (American Psycho-logical Association, 1996).

Children are also at special risk for exposure to stressors that lie outside of most adults' experience. For example, children are more likely to be traumatized by kidnapping, serious animal bites, severe injuries from burns, accidental shootings, or car ac-cidents. Children are also at particular risk for witnessing vio-lence to a family member (Amaya-Jackson & March, 1995). Traumatic stress reactions follow logically from the intense fear, horror, and helplessness with which so many children live. The effect of the trauma is further compounded if children don't re-ceive sufficient comforting and protection in the aftermath of an overwhelming experience.

Millions of children each year feel unsafe at home, at school, and in their communities. They are emotionally, physically, and sexually abused, neglected, homeless, hungry, unable to focus or learn, and victims of and witnesses to terrifying violence. They let us know, through their silence, that they cannot speak about such unfathomable evil. Such compelling observations should shake the very foundation of therapy with children and adoles-cents. We first must create a safe place for these kids so they get back on the runway once again. We'll be even more effective if we also extend our interventions beyond the confines of the therapy room; for children to develop, they've got to have child-hoods.

3

One Thing
to Cheer About

THE PRIMARY EMPHASES OF no-talk therapy—someone to feel close to and something to feel proud of—are child-sized versions of Freud's (1930) assertion that adult civilization is founded upon "the power of love" and "the compulsion to work" (p. 48). The mature capacity for love and work ordinarily begins to develop in childhood, with nurturing relationships and meaningful activities. But no-talk kids are usually handicapped in both areas; they expect both rejection and failure. By the time they are referred for therapy, they may already be quite "uncivilized," spending their days on the social and structural periphery. No one is cheering for them, and they don't expect that anyone will. When their lack of competence is paired with an unsupportive environment, they're at enormous risk of drifting even further towards the margins as time goes on.

SOMEONE TO FEEL CLOSE TO

The relationship rules in no-talk therapy. Without a connection, there is no treatment. These kids need us more than they are ever likely to acknowledge. No-talk kids have usually experienced a significant disruption in normal development. This disruption invariably has a dramatic interpersonal effect. They typically feel unempowered and disconnected from others. Healing, therefore, is based upon a realistic sense of self-control and the creation of new connections. Such recovery can only take place within the context of relationships; it cannot occur in isolation. For this reason, therapy can become just the right intervention.

In a similar vein, Erik Erikson (1963) describes the ego structures that kids must develop from infancy through adolescence. These include the basic capacities for trust, initiative, competence, and identity. Just as these capabilities are originally stunted by destructive relationships with other people, so must they be reformed through supportive relationships.

Moreover, one of the most consistent findings in the resiliency literature is the presence of a caring adult in the life of the child or adolescent. Resilient adults, who have survived horrendous and traumatic experiences during childhood, almost always had someone to whom they were especially close (e.g., Cohler, 1987; Garmezy, 1983; Olson, 1993; Steele, 1986; Werner, 1989; Zimrim, 1986). This involved adult doesn't have to spend a great deal of time with the child or adolescent, but the relationship has to be maintained over an extended period. Werner (1988) concludes that, "Our research on resilient children has shown us that they had at least one person in their lives who accepted them unconditionally regardless of temperamental idiosyncrasies, physical attractiveness, or intelligence" (p. 5). *Never* undervalue the importance of the therapeutic relationship, because it may be the most vital link to survival the no-talk kid has. Coming to therapy may, in fact, be the first thing to cheer about.

The Therapeutic Relationship

People outside of the realm of child therapy find our work mysterious and amusing. Building with Legos, playing Candyland, making watercolor paintings, and writing stories on the com-

puter hardly sound like real work. Indeed, few of our contem-
poraries know more about getting clay out of the rug than we
do. Therapists specializing in work with adults exude poise and
confidence (and get many fewer runs in their stockings; they
also don't generally have a finely developed hook shot from
mid-room with a Nerf ball, but these are just details). Therapists
of adult clients also have simpler theories of how therapy works,
and their strategies for intervention tend to make developmental
sense. They hear gratifying phrases like, "I thought a lot about
what we talked about last week and this is what I'd like to work
on today. . ." and are seldom greeted by silence. They can treat
someone for months without ever speaking to anyone else about
the client, save, perhaps, a managed-care administrator. Why
would anyone want to be a child therapist?

Like the younger sibling in a large family, child therapists
have to assert themselves loudly and firmly. We have to be able
to justify our work to parents, others on the team, managed
care, and the kids themselves. This represents a fairly constant
barrage of explanations about what it is we do and why. "Yes,
we 'just played with Lincoln Logs today,'" we say, "but this
activity involves sharing materials, feelings about home, and
problem-solving, and we're building a therapeutic relationship."
"No, I can't 'just ask Sue if her father abuses her on visits,'" we
almost apologize, "she lacks the cognitive and emotional maturity to make sense of such a question. But I am alert and responsive to themes of safety and danger in her play with the
bear family. . . ." And the justifications do not stop until they
go all the way around the circle and back to ourselves—as we
review our case plan, and the things we do that distinguish us
from other well-intentioned adults. What then does make the
therapeutic relationship different from all of the others in a
child or adolescent's life?

Although process research on child therapy is surprisingly
limited, it is quite likely that the therapeutic relationship is helpful to kids in much the way all good social relationships are.
Sometimes we may feel, accurately, as though we are helping
lonely or alienated kids simply by being there for them. We can

see how our healthy "reparenting" provides more positive models and connections for kids from dysfunctional environments. However, good therapy goes well past warm friendship or high-class babysitting in several essential ways.

First, in therapy we use the relationship *intentionally* as a vehicle for change. Hans Strupp (1986) has described psychotherapy as "the systematic use of a human relationship" (p. 513). Unlike other social encounters that are intended as a means to something (e.g., learning to read, playing a sport), the therapeutic connection is, in some part, the point of it all. In fact, the lack of strong research evidence supporting one therapeutic technique over another may be attributable to the fact that *who* we are in therapy is more important than *what* we do.

Second, the therapeutic relationship serves as the scaffolding onto which development of competencies, self-esteem, problem-solving, self-soothing, and the whole business of therapy are hung. Additionally, as Shirk and Russell (1996) have pointed out, the therapist also *scaffolds* by helping the child function within the therapeutic partnership at a slightly higher level than he would by himself. In successful child and adolescent therapy, we help kids experience their *potential* developmental level through our support. This can be manifested concretely in building a car model that comes out nicely or in successfully negotiating a later curfew. It is also inherent in the subjective experience that kids have when they feel socially competent with us. In this way, the therapeutic relationship serves as a kind of link between ordinary and optimal functioning for kids.

Third, the therapeutic relationship must operate as a kind of special alliance to be successful. The safety and specialness of therapy are paramount. The concept of a therapeutic alliance isn't, by any means, new. What is different now is the extent to which we must defend this alliance against technique-laden approaches that view the therapeutic relationship as something to be gotten through so the "real work" can begin.

Because many no-talk kids bring a horrendous history of disappointing, punishing, and abandoning relationships to therapy, the formation of a working alliance can be a full-time job. In fact, their past experiences guarantee that not much else will be accomplished until they can see the therapist as something of an ally in the big fight for survival. While therapeutic techniques are of tremendous value in some situations, they necessarily take a back-burner position while the establishment of basic trust proceeds. A good relationship is not merely the precursor to therapy but, in many ways, the very point of treatment with no-talk kids.

A fourth distinction of the therapeutic relationship, then, is how the connection itself brings about change for kids. Many theorists argue that psychopathology arises as a result of troubled social experiences, which are then internalized. Children with emotional and behavioral problems have developed a core set of beliefs about themselves and the world that stem from the social problems they've had (e.g., Bowlby, 1988; Safran, 1990; Strupp, 1989). For some kids, therefore, the goals of therapy are entirely interpersonal. From this perspective, the relationship itself can be viewed as a kind of technique to enhance social development.

Therapy with no-talk kids provides them with a new way to be with an adult. Since they are prepared for us to be inattentive, harsh, and rejecting, as others have been in the past, they need to see how different we can be. By being with them in a present, empathic, accepting way, for example, we weaken the expectations that have contributed to their misery. At the same time, our relationship serves as a kind of in vivo experiment in becoming more socially successful elsewhere. For kids who have had a lifetime of interpersonal failure and pain, the mending power of a therapeutic connection can be profound and transformative.

SOMETHING TO FEEL PROUD OF

The facts are irrefutable: Kids who have a track record of success are more likely to believe they can succeed the next time a challenge comes around. But kids need to hear the upbeat "can do" message from others—and also believe it themselves. (We can't be the only ones cheering; it has to be *their* truth, too.) Two determinants can create self-esteem in children and adolescents: authentic approval from significant others *and* competence in domains of importance to them (Harter, 1993).

The five areas that children and adolescents cite as most important are: school achievement, athletic skill, peer acceptance, good behavior and physical attractiveness (not necessarily in that order) (Harter, 1993). The majority of kids in the cultural mainstream share these values and know that their peers and parents do, too. The relationship between experiences of success in these domains and self-esteem is well documented and has some clear implications for good no-talk therapy.

School Achievement

The fact that kids spend so much of their lives at school would be reason enough for us to want this to be a successful experience for them. But clearly, academic achievement has implications that far exceed feeling good during the day. Our society places a premium on scholastic competence, and the job market holds little promise for kids who do poorly in school or drop out. Much is riding on school performance for both self-esteem and a chance at a future. Arguably, since the structure of school (and our society) is competitive, some kids will always be losers—that's the way it's set up. In a system that can only have some winners, no-talk kids will need plenty of support to overcome a legacy of failure.

Especially if they are also quiet at school, no-talk kids often fall through the cracks, perhaps sliding by with the minimum of effort and learning what can keep them from flunking. Or they may fail on a grand scale, with little investment in changing things and even fewer skills for doing so. Given the range of attention and learning problems these kids often have, it is critical that no-talk therapy involve itself in changing the school experience. Kids may benefit from testing, tutoring, having an individualized education plan, classroom consultation, referral to a different school or program, or a multitude of other productive interventions designed to meet their compelling academic needs.

Sometimes the fit between the child and his teacher is poor. While no-talk kids often elicit negative reactions from staff, this response is often quite specific—a mismatch of personalities. A teacher who particularly likes obedience will be less pleased with a defiant child than a teacher who is unfazed by such challenges. But even quiet kids can have problems with certain teachers.

For example, Alan, an anxious seven-year-old foster child, was assigned a rigid second grade teacher who was extremely particular about compliant and orderly behavior in his class. This was the only second grade teacher in the small, rural school, so the match had to work. Terrified, Alan was unable to speak up when called on and panicked when he had to complete assignments. He was sure the work would be inadequate. In fact, his papers *were* a mess, covered with smudges and erasures. The teacher saw Alan's paralysis and messiness as stubborn resistance. But Alan had begun nervously chewing his fingertips and his outbursts at home were increasing. I accompanied Alan's foster parents to a meeting at the school. The teacher, it turned out, had no idea of Alan's history, but also felt he couldn't treat the boy differently than his 27 classmates. Following some testing to assess his level of distress, Alan was assigned an aide in the classroom who sat near him and helped him manage his anxiety so he could learn in school. The year improved rapidly for this child after these modifications were made.

If a teacher doesn't like a particular child or adolescent, the set-up for failure is established. In such cases, we need to work with kids, parents, and schools to help them recognize the poor fit and, if possible, arrange for a better match. Even when a change of teachers is not possible, we can devise ways to buffer children so that they also have successful relationships in school.

Athletic Skill

Sports and aerobic activities share many beneficial functions for kids. The relationship between exercise and emotional well-being has been persuasively established. Kids who play sports and participate in physical activity tend to engage in other mainstream activities. And although highly competitive sports (with an unhealthy emphasis on winning) can result in excessive levels of stress, less rigorous involvement appears to be associated with greater self-confidence and self-discipline, to decrease delinquent activity, and to provide a more appropriate channel for aggression (e.g., Reppucci, 1987; Segrave & Chu, 1978). Aerobic exercise is also essential for helping traumatized children and adolescents manage their intense states of anxiety.

For no-talk kids, especially, a physical outlet can boost self-esteem without reliance on conversation. Physical activity after school reduces TV time, increases social opportunities, and develops a sense of physical competence. For kids who do not want to participate in school athletics, intramurals, or community-organized sports, we need to consider other opportunities for physical activity, like rock climbing, rollerblading, yoga, tai chi, dancing, martial arts, hiking, biking, skateboarding, swimming, or orienteering. For example, Ryan, an obese and angry 12-year-old no-talk kid, seemed to be transformed on top of a horse specially trained to handle tough children. No-talk kids tend to participate in as few extracurricular activities as they can manage, and their self-esteem suffers accordingly.

Peer Acceptance

"In groups" and "popular kids" have been around for generations and show little sign of evolving or, better yet, disappearing. Such patterns seem impervious to adult intervention. Our only hope is to send more confident and resilient kids into the fray. If the available peer group seems impenetrable, then a no-talk therapy goal can be to find another group that is better suited to the child or adolescent. For example, one no-talk boy, a pudgy ten-year-old Bobby Fischer in sweat pants, was ostracized by classmates for his interest in chess and the way he dressed. Part of his no-talk therapy was arranging for him to participate in the chess club of a neighboring school. The goal should not be to reshape the child to be popular in some phony way, but to match him with a peer group more apt to accept him. The social skills he acquires in one situation are also likely to generalize as his self-esteem grows.

Good Behavior

Even though some no-talk kids are loath to admit it, most children and adolescents do want to behave well, win adult approval, and generally fit in. Kids who are in control of their own behavior also feel better about themselves. But no-talk kids typically enter therapy with a firm belief that they have *not* been behaving well—a sentiment that is underscored profoundly by parents and teachers. Many of these kids, though, are truly doing the best they can within their developmental limitations and environmental constraints.

We tend to overreact to kids who misbehave, especially if we believe that they would shape up if they knew who was boss. But it makes no sense to believe that kids who behave badly—cheating, lying, clowning, bullying, avoiding, denying, quitting, making excuses, blaming, needling, whining, arguing, not-talking—are freely choosing to be this obnoxious. It is much more likely that they have come up with a few self-defeating behaviors and lack the skill or self-confidence to develop better strategies for coping.

In a wonderful adaptation of the old adage "pick your battles," Ross Greene (1998) describes a "three basket" approach to dealing with kids whose problem-solving techniques are, at best, chronically inflexible, and who behave in noncompliant or explosive ways. This strategy works extremely well in no-talk therapy, where we attend to successes and ignore as many problems as we can.

In the first basket, we put (and encourage parents and teachers to share our choices) those requirements of life that we absolutely insist upon—for reasons of health or safety, for example. For basket-one issues, we will not back down or negotiate and will maintain the expectation that the child or adolescent will comply, no matter what it takes to get him to do so. Basket one can include only expectations that are realistic, though. The child has to be capable of success in these on a fairly consistent basis, *and* we have to be willing and able to enforce the basket-one requirements.

In the second basket we'll put more questionable issues, ones that only *might* be worth fighting for. And before we draw any line in concrete on these we should think about less severe strategies for handling them. We may, instead, negotiate, compromise, brainstorm, talk it over, or offer alternatives—anything to avoid another hopeless mess, meltdown, or failure for us all. In terms of conflict over questionable behavior, with no-talk kids we keep basket one as empty as possible, and try basket-two strategies more often. This may mean we help families compromise on a later curfew, that we don't worry as much about school issues for a bit until another area of success is cooking along, or that we suggest that parents do their child's laundry chores to eliminate this area of conflict for now.

Basket three, as may seem obvious by now, will be filled to overflowing. We'll help parents and school to put aside former struggles in the name of harmony and better behavior the rest of the time. For example, some parents choose to include clean rooms, balanced meals, and combed hair in this, the most trivial basket. Similarly, schools may modify assignments and give kids a place to go to read instead of attending all their classes. We fill basket three to acknowledge our understanding that life is too hard for no-talk kids. We want them to be less frustrated and angry; reducing the number of demands on them is an important way to help them feel better.

The main point is that, when kids expect to fail, they will behave miserably. In turn, our harsh or punitive reactions to them serve only to perpetuate this expectation. No-talk kids need to get off the hook for a while and to have more time when their behavior is not being questioned or challenged. Until they have fewer struggles, we will not be able to provide them with the time and space they require for learning more adaptive and planful behaviors and improving their self-esteem.

This theory of three baskets runs counter to most conventional parenting wisdom, which holds kids accountable more of the time. But no-talk kids are not conventional in managing their lives. It follows that we need to develop new explanations and strategies that will work for them, even if it means lowering the "expectations bar" to the toddler level and changing the dialogue altogether.

Physical Attractiveness

Of the values that kids share, physical attractiveness is probably the one least amenable to psychotherapy. But it remains of critical interest, since it is the domain by far the most predictive of self-esteem, especially for girls. Harter's (1993) studies show correlations between high self-esteem and feelings of attractiveness between .70 and .80. Of course, we can hook overweight kids up with an aerobics class, or recommend an orthodontist or dermatologist for kids with specific problems, but these surface solutions may not be sufficient to alter low self-esteem that stems from a deeply felt belief in one's own ugly appearance—a belief that's based purely in *subjective* truth.

This is a tremendously potent problem, and one associated with the multitude of difficulties for which girls (and some boys) enter therapy: depression, suicide, sexual acting-out, drug use and eating disorders, for example. Our best bet is often to help these kids shape a more complex and rich identity, with other competencies and interests, while focusing our rage on the hideous, superficial culture around us that does this to so many of our children.

Most of the research to date shows that self-esteem is not as easy to change as we'd like. Windows of opportunity seem to open during times of transition (e.g., shift from elementary to middle to high school, in new circumstances). Advances in self-perception become feasible when the child or adolescent has different developmental tasks to master or a new reference group with which she can compare herself (Harter, 1993).

According to research findings about self-esteem, therapy *can* serve a couple of useful functions. First, it can help kids create and use transition points in their lives. To boost self-esteem, we can match a child's abilities and what she values with actual opportunities. This may be as simple as finding some after-school computer classes for a web-whiz, doing art projects with an aspiring Picasso, or finding a rec-league soccer team that has enough other beginners so a child can fit in. The goal is to tailor self-esteem to a *realistic sense of hope* about achieving in a new environment. No-talk kids sometimes come to us after years of frustration and failure. They need help trying again in yet another situation. No-talk therapy can also have an impact on self-esteem by helping these kids develop new social networks that can provide greater sources of approval. For many, successful social experiences may be the most useful intervention we can provide.

FOSTERING COMPETENCE IN KIDS

Happily, contemporary trends in psychotherapy have shifted away from exclusive emphasis on psychopathology and now also pay attention to strengths, resources, coping, and areas of competence. We have to give no-talk kids some skills and success or they won't stay in treatment. As Robert Brooks (1994) has commented:

> Because of their low self-esteem, many at-risk children seem to find themselves drowning in an ocean of inadequacy. However,

every child has "islands of competence," areas that are (or could be) sources of pride and accomplishment. As part of the intervention strategy, parents, teachers, and other significant adults in the child's life can identify and reinforce these islands of competence; doing so may create a ripple effect, motivating the child to venture forth and confront the tasks that have been difficult. (p. 549)

Fostering competence in kids is at the heart of our cheerleading. It is based on four enveloping principles that are, not coincidentally, as true for our own lives as for the kids we treat.

Finding Meaning

The work we do in no-talk therapy has got to have meaning for everyone in the therapy room. We need to convey to kids that we are *committed* to making it work, here and now. The meaning we construct proceeds from the belief that if we were this kid, in the family, school, and community she inhabits, we would do exactly as she is doing now. Kids can be tremendously relieved to know that we are accepting them at their exact developmental and behavioral place. They are starving for meaning, for value, for something real to sink their teeth into. Our work, or our own kids at home, or the hiking we do on the weekends, may provide meaning for us. What has meaning for them? Where *do* they succeed? What are they committed to?

Rising to the Challenge

Similarly, no-talk therapy provides a series of opportunities to rise to a challenge. We can convey to these kids that our own frustration and inadequacy and sense of impending doom can be put to good use. For example, we can get some live consultation when we get stuck in therapy; the no-talk kid can watch us seek out resources, confess our fallibility, and problem solve. We get to model our vision for change as a positive experience. No-talk therapy then becomes an occasion for new learning, feeling better, becoming more effective for *them*. After all, therapy is their challenge as well. Resilient kids see obstacles as inevitable parts of life—not as causes of irrevocable defeat. How can we use therapy to give no-talk kids the strength to try again on their way to attainable goals? How do we ensure that challenges can also lead to successes?

Controlling Ourselves

No-talk kids believe that they have little or no control over their lives. They are preserving their self-esteem and dignity in the only way they know how. We may view their behavior as intentionally provocative and challenging and attempt to wrest that meager control away from them. What we *should* do is try to control ourselves and what *we* do. We offer them rare validation by respecting their struggle to take hold of their own lives.

Without a sense of ownership and responsibility for their behavior, no-talk kids are at risk for serious problems. As a corollary, most researchers who have studied competence note that personal control serves as the basic scaffolding for self-esteem, motivation, and resilience (e.g., Anthony & Cohler, 1987; Brooks, 1994; Deci & Chandler, 1986). An accurate appraisal of what we can control is critical in no-talk therapy (as in life). Our job, therefore, is to maintain our own sense of control within the sessions. Good no-talk therapy provides lots of opportunities for kids to run the show, too.

Staying Cautiously Optimistic

Competent people are an optimistic lot. They tend to bounce back from failures with a plan for how to make it better next time. In studies that distinguish resilient kids from their more vulnerable peers, researchers describe an "optimistic bias"—the resilient kids latch onto any excuse for hope and faith that things will get better (e.g., Murphy, 1987). Echoing this, Bruno Bettelheim wrote, "We all survive on trust and hope, not on fact" (Bettelheim & Rosenfeld, 1992, p. 4).

But no-talk kids do not necessarily share this enthusiasm, at least up front. They point to the facts of their lives as evidence that things are pretty hopeless. Sitting with them can make us feel similarly overwhelmed; it's hard to be upbeat when you're being sneered at or a kid is tearing your office apart. But fostering competence in kids means nurturing whatever microscopic hope they have managed to keep alive. Our cautious optimism about therapy's usefulness provides the context in which other kinds of confidence can grow.

No-Talk Goals

What we do with kids makes them feel more successful and closer to us. By contrast, the way we *think* about our goals sets us further apart. Our arcane theories and complex intervention strategies distance us from their experience of childhood. Psychological formulations and insights are the hallmark of good adult work, but abstraction undermines what needs to happen in a child therapy session.

We certainly need to devise thoughtful, conceptually sound treatment goals, but these are too often taken from adult formulae: "reduce depression utilizing cognitive-behavioral techniques," "detriangulate child from acrimonious parental dyad through strategic family interventions," or "increase self-esteem using solution-focused discussions." The recipient of these often carefully considered objectives may well be an inarticulate seven-year-old who is having trouble learning to read and senses his parents are on the verge of divorce. In no-talk therapy, since kids are small, our immediate goals can be, too. There is no need for therapy to replicate those 18th-century primitive paintings in which kids looked like miniature adults.

Goal-setting must include the child or adolescent, and can be developed through a written contract or a shared understanding. Goals should be short-range, to ensure frequent revision, and simple, only gradually revealing the shape of things to come:

- "We'll play games, and I'll give you a couple of good relaxation strategies."
- "I'll help you find a job, and do some tests that can tell us why you're hating math so much."
- "You'll go to Alateen and then tell me why you're different from the other kids there."
- "I'll teach you how to play poker, and you'll show me how many ways you can shoot the Nerf ball into the basket."
- "Eventually, we'll do some negotiating with your parents to get you a later curfew."
- "Maybe someday you won't melt down so quickly."
- "How about trying out for that school play?"

It may seem obvious that life is made up of millions of little experiences; the minutiae in our own memories is evidence of that. (Remember that favorite teacher's smile, or the smell of grandma's apple pie? How about that time you sent a message in a bottle out to sea? What is the story behind the scar on your chin? Is there enough milk in the fridge?) But child therapists get so bogged down in technique that we forget what we know at an intuitive level.

No-talk goals transform like sap turns into maple syrup. Lots of little projects and games get distilled, over time, into something quite wonderful. The transition is really a metamorphosis, in which the no-talk goals change appearance as objectives evolve from immediate to long-term, and from concrete to abstract. Like good parents, we need to keep in mind how the small stuff—some enthusiasm and cooing, and a satisfying activity or two—can provide the "sap" for a confident and successful "Grade A" kid to emerge. Table 1 illustrates this idea.

Table 1. Sweet Goals

Maple Sap	*into*	*Maple Sugar*
Show up every Tuesday at 2:00		Build trust and consistency
Do hypnotic exercise: e.g., floating on a safe cloud		Increase self-soothing
Play poker		Build relationship, have fun
Make and eat peanut-butter crackers		Share in a project, nurture
Paint a poster for the wall		Increase self-esteem
Shoot hoops all around room		Increase flexible problem-solving
Arrange a ropes course		Provide links to success
Get a later curfew		Model negotiation skills
Make clay "family" figures		Develop symbolic play skill

THE CHEERFUL THEMES OF NO-TALK THERAPY

In no-talk therapy, less really is more. As in marriage, where the little things like replacing toilet paper and doing dishes can make intimacy possible, so the small activities we do with kids can have great impact. Things to cheer about can come in all kinds of packages, as shown below.

Developing Wonder

No-talk kids don't have wonderful lives in any sense of the expression. Somewhere along the line, they became less curious

than other kids, not given to "wonder." Through this same process, they stopped feeling hopeful about themselves and their
chances. But without wonder, the problem-solving strategies of
no-talk kids remain rigid and undeveloped. The excitement that
typical children feel at the first snowfall, or watching a card
trick, or when a theater gets dark before the curtain goes up,
leads them to become more inquisitive. When we are open to
wonder, we can begin to anticipate the unknown with interest,
rather than dread.

No-talk therapy can become a rich landscape of anticipation
once we become tuned into it. Any activity that holds a particle
of interest can be "wonderful." In the process, of course, kids
begin to develop problem-solving and planning skills they need
desperately. For example:

- Wonder how many ways a ball can go in the basket?
- Wonder what happens if I cheat at cards and don't get
  caught—or cheat and do?
- Wonder who will step on untied shoelaces during our walk
  and whether anyone will trip and fall down?
- Wonder how many more blocks can go on the tower before
  it will collapse?
- Wonder how many more classes can be skipped before the
  teacher notices?
- Wonder how the pudding will taste with all these lumps?
- Wonder whether the picture should go on the wall or go home?
- Wonder what will happen to the Little Pig when the Big
  Bad Wolf huffs and puffs?
- Wonder who would be most surprised if the math assign-
  ment got handed in?

Encouraging Contributions

Children need lots of chances to assume those responsibilities
that will foster a sense of ownership and pride in their home,
school, and communities. The experience of making a positive

difference in the lives of others not only builds self-respect and hopefulness but also serves as a powerful antidote to feelings of defeat and despair (Brooks, 1991, 1994).

In the course of no-talk therapy, contributions go both ways; kids get the chance to contribute to the therapist's well-being, too. We all need to know we can make a difference in the quality of someone's life. Kids can water plants, make photocopies, microwave popcorn, plant seeds for a windowbox, stamp letters, sort out old Magic Markers, or decorate a wall. Why must we professionals be the only ones who get to help?

One small boy without many skills became my ace Xeroxer, faxer, and stapler. I'd save documents all week just for him. He even began correcting me about the best way to send things: "You'll have to make a copy of this first. The folded part will make it stick in the fax." Though it may seem like a small intervention, he knew I needed him, too.

Staying Positive

An important aspect of our job is noticing the little differences, providing encouragement, going for the constructive reframe, and generally understanding that these kids are acting this way for legitimate reasons. We need to be genuinely upbeat in order to foster realistic hope. We need to believe that we can help and that therapy will be a good experience for the no-talk kid. Our positive tone has to extend beyond the individual therapy sessions into other activities, including notes to the the kids in the mail and family meetings. Our ability to stay positive also gives no-talk kids a sense of belonging when they come to our offices. We need to be sure they feel welcome, with right-sized furniture and activities and food *they* like.

Our responses to no-talk kids embrace their spirit, determination, and coping strategies. We say *"and"* instead of *"but"* when we suggest what else they might do, indicating that their *efforts* are also commendable. We may tell them, "I love your spirit, *and* your style needs some work," or, "You're very brave to resist all these adults telling you what to do, *and* I see some other ways to handle them that we could try." We notice any little thing that indicates skill or effort: "Did you plan ahead to save the Uno Wild Card for the end? That was a great strategy." "You hung in for the whole hour today; that was impressive." Our underlying message is: I'll help you fine-tune that voice so people can hear what you're trying to say. I'll support you in developing the skills you'll need to feel better. We're all doing the best we can.

Fostering Self-Discipline

Self-discipline helps kids stay out of trouble, boosts self-esteem, gives them resources to cope with adversity and stress, and contributes to resilience. In short, developing a sense of internal control is fundamental to success in life. But no-talk kids tend to act before thinking. They have difficulty planning in a realistic way, seldom considering what will happen next—to them or to other people. In turn, they can't figure out how to act differently next time.

Without self-discipline, we are all condemned to make the same mistakes over and over again. (As the saying goes, the goal of therapy is to help people stop experiencing the same damn thing all the time, so they can then encounter one damn thing after another.) No-talk therapy can help kids develop self-discipline through a variety of methods:

- Involve kids in designing their own consequences for misbehavior.
- Have them help develop realistic rules and expectations.
- Put plans in writing and have them co-sign the document.
- Get them out into the world of work and nurturing.
- Always ask for their feedback and input.
- Explain the purpose of rules before imposing them.
- Keep the number of basket-one expectations to a minimum.
- Rely on natural consequences, especially with older kids.
- Help kids learn their arousal signals and develop self-soothing strategies.

Increasing Compassion

Our empathic connection with no-talk kids is the foundation for their own developing ability to see themselves as likeable and worthy. No-talk kids, especially those who have been traumatized, have notable deficits in empathizing with the needs and feelings of others (Pearce & Pezzot-Pearce, 1997). They may not have developed compassion because of the absence of reciprocity and sharing in their lives. Or they may become overwhelmed by someone else's pain because it reminds them of their own psychological distress. No-talk therapy helps kids develop compassion and perspective-taking through:

- Playing games that require taking turns, and winning and losing.
- Playing games that have no winners or losers.
- Helping kids identify their own needs in different situations.
- Looking at pictures of people in different situations and then discussing how the people are feeling.
- Role-playing.
- Modeling empathic behavior.
- Identifying universal feelings that people may have in different situations (e.g., being abused, failing a test, having a birthday party).
- Putting on puppet shows.
- Talking about "friendly deeds" that kids can do.

Making Mistakes

No-talk kids have a harsher reaction to making mistakes than the rest of us do. They see the recurring mess-ups in their lives as ultimate proof of their unworthiness, as opposed to the inevitable lumps and curves in life. Of course, we will, without even trying, find ways to model imperfection for them brilliantly. But, like good parents, no-talk therapists are pragmatic about mistakes; we can look at "spilled milk" without excitement or undue concern. We know that these kids are easily embarrassed and defeated, but that, without mistakes, people don't learn as much. Robert Brooks (1994) describes a classroom teacher who would have worked well with no-talk kids:

> At the beginning of the school year, the teacher asked which of the students thought they would probably make a mistake or not understand something in class that year. Before any of the children could respond, the teacher raised his own hand. Then the teacher asked the students why they thought he had asked the question. He used their answers as the starting point for a discussion of the ways in which the fear of mistakes and embarrassment limits the freedom to offer opinions and learn. (p. 552)

In no-talk therapy, we can help kids deal more comfortably and effectively with their mistakes by being willing to talk about our own (being late, messy, forgetting the new paints, etc.), and using other therapy techniques, including:

- Awarding "Fresh Start" certificates to them after a mistake gets made; awarding Fresh Start certificates to ourselves, too. The Fresh Start certificate has many uses. For example, an eight-year-old boy named Ben arrived in therapy after a terrible day. He'd been in the principal's office and kicked off the bus. Ben's mother has been notified, and she dreaded the inevitable conflict about this as much as Ben did. He understood what he did that was wrong, but he was so deep in the hole that he couldn't make things better. I gave Ben a Fresh Start award, and we both signed it. This award gave him a chance to have this day erased. We called the principal, and Ben explained how he'd handle tomorrow differently. (When he arrived at school the following day, the principal shook his hand, acknowledging that the past day was forgotten.) I also gave Ben's mother a Fresh Start award so the two of them could have a peaceful evening, which they did. At times, we all have the right to act like Scarlett O'Hara and be reassured that "tomorrow is another day."

- Running the imaginary video (or a real tape) so the failed experience gets replayed the right way.
- Providing immediate successes so that kids can have both kinds of experiences.
- With younger kids, reading books about bad days like *Alexander and the Terrible Horrible No Good Very Bad Day, Curious George, Leo the Late Bloomer, Noisy Nora,* or *Where the Wild Things Are.*
- With older kids talking about Bill Clinton, Dennis Rodman, or any other famous people who have, from time to time, messed up on a grand scale (they're easy to find in the waiting room copy of *People*).
- Using humor to laugh it off.

Authoring Lives

No-talk kids usually have a tough time with traditional narrative approaches. But, like all of us, they do have an essential story to tell about who they are and the choices they make. Even if they won't or can't provide a narrative about how they became a "no-talk kid," we still need to convey to them that we see them as the authors of their own lives. And, since a fundamental goal of no-talk therapy is empowerment, we have to find methods to get them into the driver's seat and to encourage them to take seriously the notion that they can steer the car if they want. This tends to be a strange and alien idea for no-talk kids—one that can be both frightening and appealing.

The ideas of autonomy and authorship go hand-in-hand. The more kids have a sense of control over their lives, feel involved in solutions, make choices within sessions (and in the real world), the more prepared they will be to take on this authorship. No-talk kids need to know that they *have* a story to tell, even if they are not, at the outset, prepared to commit it to words.

David Epston's lovely adaptation of the narrative approach for children, particularly his technique of externalizing "symptom bullies" (Freeman, Epston, & Lobovits, 1997), is worth describing briefly. This technique separates kids from their problems. They

carve out a more constructive identity for themselves by working to resist and overcome their "bullies" (worrying, fighting,
tantrums, fears, depression—any identified symptom). Freeman,
Epston, and Lobovits suggest that activity-based therapy can
serve the narrative approach well and offer the following ideas
for a nonverbal or less verbal foray into a child's story:

- What does the problem look/seem/feel/sound like to you?
- Can you show it in a cartoon or drawing, or make a mask?
- Does it look like one of these puppets to you? Would you
  rather use puppets to talk?
- Could you show me what you mean by making a scene or
  map in the sandtray?
- Could you dance or move and show how it feels when the
  problem takes over? (p. 160)

The narrative approach directs attention to choices—to rival
narratives that could also describe the child's life. These alternative ways of telling a story may include a richer variety of events
beyond the symptoms—a story more in line with how the child
would like to be known. To contrast with the "problem-saturated
picture," the rival narratives feature the strengths, special abilities, and aspirations of the child and family. The narrative technique divides a story in two, carefully separating the relative
influences of the child and the problem. For example, when kids
create a "problem mask" they are also invited to make a "solution
mask" (Barragar Dunne, 1992). Or, when one of the puppets
turns into a "problem bully," another will enter the fray with the
child's opposing perspective. Some other strategies for authoring
lives in no-talk therapy include:

- Writing the story on the computer.
- Finishing sentence stems related to the story.
- Creating a timeline of important events and adding to it.
- Making an imaginary video or radio show and directing it.
- Writing a "menu" of choices for a given impasse.

- Making a symbolic map of the life story.
- Inventing a code so the willing child can indicate responses without speaking.

There are few feelings more wonderful than breaking through the no-talk wall; however, the principles involved are much easier to outline than to maintain in daily practice. This is hard work that we do and we won't be as successful if we do it alone.

4

The Circle of Adults

NO-TALK THERAPY CAN follow the main principles of individual, family, or community psychology. But it doesn't matter which theoretical approach is dominant in a given case—we still attend closely to the child in context. We know that we won't be able to assist in bringing about lasting change if we ignore the needs of the rest of the family and the untapped resources of the neighborhood. To paraphrase the now-clichéd expression: It really takes a village to raise a no-talk kid. In study after study, the two critical components for reaching high-risk kids are *intensive individualized attention* and *community-wide, multiagency collaboration* (see Dryfoos, 1990, for a thorough review of this literature).

As we plan our own obsolescence, we need to be certain that organizations and providers in the community can fill in where we leave off. Ideally, once a child or adolescent has forged natural links to her neighborhood, and interventions are helping the whole family function more effectively, we can become extraneous. Thus, an important part of no-talk therapy is building these enduring supports.

We are part of a "treatment team," whether we like it or not and whether we acknowledge it or not. Even if child therapists choose not to meet with parents, school administrators, pediatricians, or the lifeguard at the "Y," those other adults also have a stake in the life of the no-talk kid. And, more importantly, no-talk kids need this stable circle of adults around them.

The "circle of adults," then, can be an informal array of people and activities, a well-articulated treatment team, or some semistructured arrangement in between. In the typical situation, the no-talk kid becomes a "case" that we "manage" from our offices, coordinating services behind the scenes, meeting as needed with parents, holding family sessions, and attending school meetings. In reality, though, we are not so much case managers as Sherpas. No-talk kids and their families usually don't need to be managed so much as guided over the steep and uneven developmental terrain.

When families need more support and structure than a Sherpa guide in a loosely connected circle can provide, the concept of case management can be formalized to include other agencies and systems. At some point in caring for no-talk kids from multiproblem families, we become just another participant and the job of "case management" usually falls to someone else who has the primary role in the circle.

Usually the degree of chaos and dysfunction in a referral tells us the level our early interventions will need to take. Less complex cases will clearly need less intensive support. But the range of services a no-talk family may require can't be easily categorized. Like everything else in no-talk therapy, the nature and size of the circle of adults are dictated by the particular needs of a given child and family.

There's a world out there beyond the four walls of a therapist's office, and it is helpful to develop an ongoing list of resources that includes the numbers for church youth groups and soccer leagues as well as school guidance counselors and agencies with access to respite care. Naturally, every community has a different array of organizations and services. What follows are some ideas for the circle of adults and programs that can benefit no-talk kids.

COMMUNITY-BASED PEOPLE AND PROGRAMS

Just like no-talk therapists, community programs and the adults who run them tend to be concerned primarily with promoting competencies and general health. They recognize the many influences on the well-being of children and adolescents, including economics, education, physical health, and emotional supports. Located in neighborhoods (e.g., schools, church basements, town centers), community-based programs also have significant advantages for rural and inner-city kids who don't have easy access to mental-health clinics and hospitals. A particular circle of adults can embrace many different group leaders, from Big Sisters to ministers to soccer coaches.

Youth Organizations

National surveys of children and adolescents indicate that more than 20 percent of kids are active in community youth organizations (Davis & Tolan, 1993; Erickson, 1986). Although most organizations are largely recreational, some are more career or avocation-oriented (e.g., Junior Achievement, 4H), some are character-building (e.g., Scouts, Boys and Girls Clubs), some are politically oriented (e.g., Amnesty International, Young Democrats), some instill ethnic pride (e.g., Sons of Italy), and some are religious (e.g., Christian Youth Groups).

It is extremely rare to find a no-talk kid who participates in community groups. But the benefits of membership in youth organizations for the involved children and adolescents have been amply documented. First, a correlation has been repeatedly established between participation and level of educational aspiration and accomplishment among children and adolescents, even when researchers control for socioeconomic status, intellectual ability, and academic performance (e.g., Hanks & Eckland, 1978; Otto, 1975).

Second, longitudinal studies (e.g., Hanks, 1981) point to a relationship between participation in community- and school-based activities and later membership in voluntary organizations and political activity in adulthood (again, even when controlling for effects of education, occupation, or income). For example, Hanks (1981) found that kids who participated in the more politically oriented organizations tended to remain activist as adults. Third, children who participate in community organizations obtain competencies that they will not generally encounter at school. This point is particularly relevant, because schools actually require the development of a very narrow set of skills; if kids do poorly academically, they are apt to spend most of their days feeling like failures.

Finally, when a child participates in such groups, the circle of adults around the child and family broadens to include other generous people from the community, who are usually donating their time and expertise. Sometimes kids are able to get their siblings and parents involved as well; for example, Boy Scouts and Girl Scouts often have other active family members. It is therapeutic for no-talk kids (and, indeed, all of us) to have an identity informed by a special connection to the community in which we live.

Organized Sports and Physical Activity

Most parents believe that participation in sports is a positive outlet and helps to keep kids out of trouble. A recent comparison of children from the mid-1970s to the late 1980s concluded that there had been a significant increase in children's participation in organized sports (Achenbach & Howell, 1993). However, the massive proliferation of organized sports and recreation for children has not been matched by research to determine how beneficial all these activities are for the children involved (e.g., Repucci, 1987). Middle-class kids with overinvested parents tend to be under a lot of pressure, and some psychologists express concern that athletic competition provides just another example of this excessive stress (e.g., Elkind, 1985; Garbarino, 1995).

But no-talk kids are typically disenfranchised and alienated. They are shy or developmentally delayed. Traumatized and marginalized, many have never been on a team, worn a jersey with a number on it, sweated with the pleasure of exertion, been hugged by a coach for a good effort. It *is* likely that some children and adolescents are overprogrammed and involved in too many activities. But this is rarely the case with no-talk kids. And physical activity doesn't have to be competitive. Kids benefit from the structure, support, peer and adult contact, and the skills they may acquire taking a karate or gymnastics class, participating in recreational soccer, doing yoga or tai chi, or swimming at the "Y." Additionally, there is ample evidence that exercise is vital to keeping kids healthy and warding off illness and depression.

No-talk kids are rarely willing to participate in high-level competitive sports. But, short of the varsity team and the Babe Ruth league, most communities offer multiple opportunities for involvement that are neither too stressful nor intense. And, on balance, the socialization, skills, and fitness that may result can make a huge difference in a child's self-esteem and self-discipline.

Youth Volunteer Service Opportunities

Mobilizing older kids and adolescents to volunteer in their communities and become direct helpers of others—companions for the elderly, tutors, babysitters, or mentors for other kids—is another productive avenue for no-talk therapy. These youth service activities serve two functions: no-talk kids get to help others *and* to feel important and useful. Instead of being seen as problems who need something done *to* or *for* them, they emerge as assets to society.

Service opportunities abound at all levels of no-talk therapy, beginning with watering plants and sharpening pencils in the therapist's office. Kids may also help others like them by compiling a book of the strategies they have devised for managing a problem (e.g., Epston, White, & "Ben,"1995; Freeman, Epston, & Lobovitz, 1997). But it is in community work that voluntary service really lets them reduce feelings of isolation and alienation, increase their understanding of and connection to people in the neighborhood, and develop a sense of competence and self-worth (e.g., Davis & Tolan, 1993; Youth and America's Future, 1988).

The growing body of research on resiliency clearly demonstrates that a pivotal factor in surviving trauma is responsibility for someone else—younger siblings, grandparents, or even pets (e.g., Zimrim, 1986). Here the responsibility is more important than the relationship in promoting healing. In the same vein, Urie Bronfenbrenner and Heather Weiss (1983) have proposed a wonderful "curriculum of caring" for schools that would be ideal for teaching no-talk kids about empathy through nurturing. As Bronfenbrenner and Weiss put it:

> It is now possible for a young person to graduate from an American high school without ever having had to do a piece of work on which someone else depended. It is also possible for a young person, female as well as male, to graduate from high school, college, or university without ever having held a baby for longer than a few seconds; without ever having had to care for someone who was old, ill or lonely; without ever having had to assist another human being who needed help. Yet, all of us, sooner or later, will desperately require such comfort and care, and no society can sustain itself unless its members have learned the motivations, sensitivities and skills that such caring demands. (pp. 405–406)

The no-talk "curriculum of caring" can extend to animals and pets as well as neighbors and relatives. Kids can volunteer in the local humane society, a day-care center, or a nursing home.

They can walk an elderly neighbor's dog or shovel the walk of a handicapped relative. They can supervise their young cousins or serve as peer mediators in school. The key is to find a way for the no-talk kid to take on a helping role in the community—to become a giver of support. The adults who supervise this caring become welcome members of the circle, uniquely positioned to speak to the child's successes. Volunteering gives kids the self-esteem that is found only in being needed and respected by other children and adults.

Another kind of therapeutic volunteer work is an apprenticeship; many professionals in the community are willing to let an interested child or adolescent "tag along." No-talk kids can follow a passion and do scut work, making some valuable contacts in the process. For example, kids can apprentice at veterinary clinics, stables, radio stations, hospitals, newspapers, gas stations, theaters, kitchens, school offices, florists, and other stores or work sites. All it takes is someone willing to join the circle and give a child or adolescent a special role.

Mentor Programs

No-talk kids can also benefit from being paired with an adult "identification" figure: a mentor or Big Brother/Big Sister in the community. The concept of one-on-one mentoring has been promoted over the years as a successful intervention with youth, especially those from impoverished, inner-city areas (e.g., Davis & Tolan, 1993; Valentin, 1984). Mentors use their success in life as a way to support the no-talk kid in school, work, or parenting. They can be recruited through universities, schools, youth organizations, religious congregations, and, most often, businesses that encourage their employees to participate. Some examples of mentoring include, for example, pairing a pregnant teen with a mature woman, a failing elementary student with a college kid, or a high-risk middle-schooler with a business leader. Especially when no-talk kids come from unstable and unsupportive homes, the addition of a mentor to the circle can provide a child or adolescent with another type of role model.

While the Big Brother/Big Sister pairing is more recreational in intent, it too can offer no-talk kids outlets and opportunities to be around caring adults. Such a relationship, if sustained over time, builds beautifully on the work of no-talk therapy. These kids need lots of opportunities to practice being in safe and supportive relationships. Kids who are deprived of frequent contact with a same-sex parent, who have parents working long hours, who have been shuffled around the foster-care system or who spend too many hours alone—all of them can gain from having a Big Brother or Big Sister all to themselves.

Work Training Programs

Many commissions and panels on the status of adolescents (e.g., Children's Defense Fund, 1998; Youth and America's Future, 1988) have endorsed work experience as an integral and effective means of developing a sense of independence, bringing adolescents into closer contact with adults and teaching them skills they will need in the future . These experts conclude that work experiences also ease the often stressful transition into adult roles, making the workplace an important educational environment. For some no-talk adolescents, job-training opportunities serve as important supplements to traditional schooling, giving them a reason to stay in school or, if they drop out, access to job skills and a G.E.D.

The National Job Corps is perhaps the most visible of these programs, but many communities have youth apprenticeships, collaborative relationships between high schools and businesses, and other longer-term training options that lead to credentials in sizeable or growing occupations. Some are quite innovative: The YouthBuild Coalition (Simons, Finlay, & Yang, 1991) has programs in 35 states, with more than 200 different sites, giving kids on-the-job construction training along with high school equivalency. But any program that provides a no-talk kid with skills and success and contact with competent adults, along with some money to spend, is worth considering.

Church-Based Programs

Most churches, synagogues, and religious organizations have programs designed to address the social, emotional, and spiritual needs of children and their families. Religious institutions typically offer counseling and sponsor prevention activities in addition to providing religious services. In poor and minority neighborhoods, the church is often the most vital link to resources for community members, offering food, shelter, clothing, and community outreach as well as prayer (Freedman, 1993). Some children and adolescents who have no other extracurricular experiences may be willing to join a church youth group. Their need for spiritual connection may endure long after they've given up on the earthly kind. Religious leaders are often enthusiastic and persistent in reaching out to kids and in collaborating with the circle of adults.

Getting children and their families involved in their local church or synagogue can also bring family members together and connect them to available social supports. Reestablishing old ties, establishing stronger ties, or creating new ties to local religious institutions can provide no-talk kids with a deeper meaning for their lives and with powerful and concerned adults.

Friends and Family

Too often, child therapists don't probe enough about the significant adults already in the life of the no-talk kid. To discover who needs to be a part of the circle, we have to ask parents and their offspring alike about the extended family and friends who are "there" for them. Sometimes an aunt, a grandfather, or the lady who lives upstairs can be a valuable resource for the no-talk kid, getting him to appointments, taking him to the zoo, baking cookies, just being there. In the isolated no-talk presentation, we may miss the most obvious supports for both children and their parents. Acknowledging and consulting with these adults can strengthen the circle enormously.

Parents can also promote links to the community for the child and the rest of the family in simple but powerful ways. Family memberships in clubs, civic organizations, and recreational centers help kids to feel a part of their neighborhoods, reducing the isolation and alienation that often characterize their lives. Memberships at the zoo, botanical gardens, art museum, science museum, planetarium, or children's museum are generally not very expensive and offer regular admission as well as special family events like performances and tours. The public library is always free. These links bring families together and also connect them to their neighborhoods in a natural, nonclinical way.

THE TREATMENT TEAM

For a sizable minority of no-talk kids, the circle of adults also involves other professionals from programs and agencies around town. Sometimes we're handed the child *and* his circle—an adjudicated delinquent, a foster child, or a severely disabled kid, for example, who will already have a team of helping adults. (One such foster child greeted me by saying, "Not another lady with a smile and earrings!") At other times, we come in at the ground level and begin the task of assembling the team—made up of both community members and professionals. In all instances, though, the team is family-centered as well as child-centered. We act to support the child in his family and the family in its community.

Parents

If a child lives at home, or is likely to return there, parents are always part of the treatment team. Parents are often relieved to hear that they are team players and no longer need to shoulder sole responsibility for their child. They must ultimately own the treatment plan, though, and should have a say in the configuration of services provided to them. No matter what size the circle, parents are still the starting and ending points.

Parents need also to identify who *they* would like to have in the circle. Their friends, families of origin, therapists, drug counselors, sponsors, partners, and employers are all potential members of the team. Whether or not a child's symptoms reflect family distress, it is likely that he will make enduring changes only when the family is also getting the support it needs. Parents are usually the experts about both what their child needs and what *they* need to succeed as a family. The process of empowerment, central to no-talk therapy with kids, extends to parents as well.

Wraparound Services

Case-management models of treatment have been around for about 20 years, having followed on the heels of deinstitutionalization in the late 1970s. Later called wraparound services, these interventions were developed in response to the fragmented approach of providing separate, categorical services to children and families. Without case management, there is little coordination of supports; troubled families are aided in a piecemeal fashion, with inconsequential contact among providers and agencies. On the other hand, children and families with isolated, discrete problems don't really need major case management; an asthmatic child can see her pediatrician, and her mother can go to AA meetings, without any verbal fanfare.

When multiproblem families are treated without any kind of coordinated wraparound, interventions tend to suffer from gaps in some services, overlap of others, and competition among agencies. Thus, for example, in a case where family violence is a problem, a battered women's advocate may be helping a woman leave her batterer, child protection may be attempting to keep the family together, and the school may be coding the child emotionally handicapped, with no provider knowing much (if anything) about the other.

No-talk kids, for whom therapy is just one potentially useful service, are supported along a continuum of adult involvement. At one end, we serve as personal consultants, and, along with the physician and school teachers, provide the main supports. A child or adolescent needing a bit more help will require case *coordination*—occasional telephone conversations and meetings with other adults, perhaps. Further down the trouble road, we may see a need for case management; the child and family need more services than therapy can provide and a variety of agencies may be involved. At the far end, the most severely troubled kids, for whom staying at home and in the community is a major endeavor, will ultimately need wraparound.

The components of wraparound are constant, but the types of services that a given family requires must be individually tailored. As Donner (1997) has noted, for wraparound to work the following criteria should be met:

1. Wraparound efforts must be based in the community.

2. Services and supports must be individualized to meet the needs of children and families.

3. The process must be culturally competent and build on the unique values, preferences, and strengths of children and families.

4. Parents must be included at every level in developing the process.

5. Agencies must have access to flexible, noncategorized funding (usually a difficult thing to achieve in practice).

6. The process must be implemented on an interagency basis and be owned by the larger community.

7. Wraparound plans must include a balance of formal services and informal community and family resources.

8. The provision of services must be unconditional. If the needs of the child and family change, the child and family are not to be rejected from services. Instead, the services must be changed.

9. Outcomes must be measured. If they are not, the wrap-around process becomes merely an interesting fad.

Many professionals and agencies can be represented in a circle of adults on the way to providing formalized wraparound, with the goal of keeping kids in the community and out of alternative care. Typically, the team looks at the child's needs in the following life domains:

- *Family*: How are members functioning individually and as a unit? What in-home services and supports are needed to strengthen their ability to stay together safely? Do the parents need respite care? Could case aides help out after school? Should there be intensive home-based family therapy? What might parent advocates do? Are there other kinds of training and education that would be helpful?

- *Living situation/residence*: Is the place where the child lives supportive of safe, healthy development? Are there ways the team can help the family manage their home so it can meet their particular needs? Does the family need subsidized housing? Do the parents have access to groceries and supplies and a way to get them home? Are they integrated into the neighborhood in which they live?

- *Educational/vocational*: Is the school meeting the child's special needs? In the case of an older adolescent, what are the career/vocational plans? What supplementary services might be beneficial (tutoring, coding, resource room, other kinds of remediation)? Does a younger child need more day care? Aftercare?

- *Social/recreational*: How is the child or adolescent managing his free time? Does he have a functioning peer group? Interests and outlets? Does he need a social-skills group, a "Y" membership, more structure on the weekends? Would a Big Brother be able to take him to the park?

- *Legal*: Does the child or family have legal involvement? How are they handling the terms of their probations, court dates, contacts with law-enforcement officers? How is the communication between therapy and probation? Are there outstanding legal issues that need to be resolved? Are family members receiving legal advocacy and support?
- *Safety*: Is the child safe? Are other family members safe? What supports need to be in place to ensure continued safety from abuse, violence, and fear at home and in the community? Do parents need education and support groups, batterers groups, alcohol counseling? Does the family need conflict resolution training or communication skills? Does the child need a tighter behavioral contract?
- *Crisis Plan*: What happens when the child is no longer safe or acts out, or a child and/or family crisis occurs? What is the crisis plan? Who gets called? What are they expected to do? Having a crisis plan for crisis-prone families makes good sense and can reduce the hours spent managing emergencies.

In case management, and especially wraparound, interagency cooperation is essential. The circle of adults requires community-wide coordination of services among, for example, mental health, juvenile justice, education, social welfare, housing, civic groups, law enforcement, business leaders, physicians and many others. Such mutual participation among different providers in a community where wraparound is not established can make the difference for a no-talk kid, but it's an arduous and time-consuming affair, even when successful.

Schools

Second only to family involvement, no-talk therapy frequently depends for its success upon a good working relationship with the school. In fact, some schools provide most of the ancillary services a child or adolescent may need, from social skills groups and tutoring to after-school care, parent involvement, vocational training and even medical and dental care. In many ways, school-based interventions provide another model of case management. This way of reaching no-talk and high-risk kids makes sense; the acquisition of basic academic and social skills is essential, and deficits in these areas are at the root of most other problems kids have. In addition, school-based interventions also have proven to be highly effective in preventing delinquency, pregnancy, drug abuse, and dropping out (e.g., Dryfoos, 1990). The marginalized no-talk kid needs to have the school as an integral part of his team, whether or not it provides more than the educational services he needs.

THE THERAPIST IN THE CIRCLE

We have an important part to play in the circle, and kids benefit from the unique skills we offer them. But we can only work within the complementarity of all the roles. For example, if a child doesn't get breakfast or lunch, or is clinically depressed, or is failing all day long at school, or is being abused at home, or is smoking pot every day, our 50 minutes a week may be, at best, a harmless but meaningless gesture. Much worse, this time can offer further evidence to the child that a "helpful adult" is an oxymoron, in which case therapy becomes just another occasion for despair.

We have an obligation to no-talk kids, to the rest of the team, and to ourselves, to be clear about what we do. Because child therapy is not just an activity that can be duplicated by any nice person, we need to be confident that this relationship is indeed different and special—and integral to the functioning of the circle of adults for a particular child. In our quest to provide them with someone to be close to and something to be proud of, we offer them our perspective on connection and competence. We join the circle of adults to offer no-talk kids many paths out of silent frustration and failure into noisy, joyful success.

5

The Therapist's Job: Magician or Policeman?

CONTEMPORARY AMERICAN culture has a certain fascination with child therapy and therapists. Getting help for kids' emotional problems no longer stigmatizes and isolates as much as it once did. Our national quest for personal growth and healing envelops our children, too. The parenting industry is booming. Self-help books and support groups on healing the child within have proliferated alongside parenting manuals, workshops, magazines, and television talk shows devoted to helping *this* batch of children grow up. This outpouring of aid suggests an awareness that the risks are greater than in previous generations, and the standards higher. Anxiety seems to have joined fluoride in our water—there is much to be worried about, and so few answers that really quench the thirst to know what's best.

The mental health of kids has become the domain of professionals with diverse training experiences—psychologists, child psychiatrists, pediatricians, family practitioners, educators, counselors, social workers, speech and language pathologists, physical and occupational therapists, day-care specialists, nurses, probation officers, child protection workers, wilderness experts, coaches, and others. There's plenty of pain to go around, and most of us are quite busy. It is also evident that the more severe the situations we take on, the less support we get and the more kids there are for us to help. An obvious example can be found in the inner-city, where child protection workers and emergency room pediatricians are swamped, but even in pristine private practice cases involving tough multiproblem kids can prevail and overwhelm.

As the social support structure around children and adolescents crumbles, and as their emotional and behavioral problems worsen, the need for intensive interventions increases. It may be only a grotesque coincidence that the popular fascination with psychotherapy has grown along with an environment so hostile to children and adolescents. Or perhaps all the interest in individual deviance and treatment helps to shift the focus away from policies that might assist kids at a broader level. This is not a novel observation; William Ryan was making the case that we blame poverty on its victims more than 25 years ago (Ryan, 1971). But since that time life for many kids has gotten significantly harder, sadder, poorer—and more perilous. So now we're also holding children responsible for their emotional and behavioral problems, *and* we're probing their pathologies—one kid at a time. But helping kids live successfully in impossible environments enables us to do little about the sources of their distress. In these worst cases, we are no more than combat doctors, patching up the soldiers to go back to the front lines. One of the most sobering aspects of working with no-talk kids is how convincingly they force us to look in the mirror and see our inadequacy for the task.

The combination of hope (for the transformational powers of therapy) and despair (about the deteriorating mental health of kids) has led child therapy down a dangerous path. Often, when all else has failed, therapists, like the shamans we aren't, imbued with powers we don't have, are called upon to do magic. No matter that the problems involve family, school, neighborhood, culture, social policy—and a child so disenfranchised that he won't even speak. A mother weeps on the phone, a school counselor calls, frantic. A probation officer or a child protection worker with 60 other cases beseeches us for help. Forgetting our wands at home, we assemble our clinking vials of weak potions and set to work. We genuinely want to make a difference and to do it quickly.

In many cases, we have five or ten sessions per year to cast our spell, though we can always hope for a few more. The cognitive-behavioral and solution-focused theories provide brief packages for us to accomplish much in the available hours, and we set to work, with specific goal-oriented questions, systematic treatment plans, externalized symptoms, and skillful assignments. These techniques can work, especially with motivated kids from invested families. They succeed when children and adolescents are willing and able to talk about their problems and follow the path for change set by the therapist. But all these techniques are lost on no-talk kids. For them we are not the Wizard of Oz, but the bumbling, (though well-intentioned) old man behind the curtain. It's a daunting, if not impossible, task to effect lasting change with a no-talk kid in a short time.

The truth is, our training could not possibly prepare us for the degree of multisystemic dysfunction and misery we are seeing. We need some power tools in our toolboxes, and all we have are the same rusty pliers that have been around for decades now, along with a few clever innovations adapted from adult treatment. Sometimes we manage to make a difference and our confidence creeps up. Then a kid saunters in, sits down, and glowers for a 50–minute eternity. Suddenly, we know nothing.

ASK THE EXPERTS

Effective no-talk therapy has its roots in this feeling of powerlessness. However, such humility has no place in the age of Ask the Experts. Juvenile sex offenders, usually with their own histories of horrendous abuse, need "therapy." Neglected and abused kids bounced among foster homes do, too. So do survivors of divorce, death, chronic illness, suicide, earthquakes, and abductions. This is not to say that therapy is worthless in these complex situations, but rather that it is no elixir for all that goes wrong in the lives of children. And, as others feel helpless in the face of immense horror and grief, so the value of therapy increases. Once we don the hat of expert, so much is expected of us. This pressure to perform wonders has its roots in the evolving nature of child therapy and the growing role of the child therapist.

Child Therapy

Child treatment, as we know it, isn't even a century old. It originated with two cases, marking the beginning of both play therapy and behavior therapy. Freud's (1909) psychoanalytic treatment of "Little Hans" was really a primitive form of no-talk therapy. Freud consulted with the boy's father without ever actually speaking directly to Little Hans. However, this intervention was a precursor to psychodynamic child-play therapy. Another early therapy case involved systemic desensitization to furry objects in a phobic three-year-old boy called "Little Peter" (Jones, 1924). This case has been heralded as the earliest behavioral intervention with a child; it has led to the set of therapies demonstrating how childhood problems can be solved without undue attention to unconscious process and discussion.

Now there are well over 230 methods of psychosocial interventions for kids—and this is a conservative estimate (Kazdin, 1988). Since these first articles were published early in the century, the two original trees have developed mighty branches with interesting buds on them. The psychodynamic approach has yielded, for example, therapies for internal conflicts and deficiencies in parenting (e.g., Freud, 1968). Client-centered methods have been developed for enhancing self-esteem (e.g., Axline, 1947) and emotional expression (e.g., Rogers, 1942).

Cognitive theories have led to treatments of cognitive distortions, cognitive deficits, and enhancing social problem-solving (e.g., Beck, 1976). Behavioral models have led to an array of therapies, including operant conditioning, modeling, cognitive-behavioral, and social-skills-training interventions (e.g., Bandura, 1977). These branches, in turn, have many of their own offshoots, including the more recent narrative (e.g., Freeman, Epston, & Lobovits, 1997), systemic, and solution-focused approaches (e.g., Selekman, 1997), along with an astonishing variety of other family and group methods.

These many approaches vary along three dimensions (Shirk & Russell, 1996). First, child therapies differ in *focus*. At one extreme, treatment attends solely to the process in the therapy room; these tend to be the more psychodynamic, client-centered methods. At the other extreme, therapy is exclusively problem-oriented; intervention is aimed at a specific therapeutic goal. The second dimension describes the degree of therapeutic *structure* imposed. On one side, the therapist provides the supportive conditions that allow the child to direct the therapy sessions; on the contrasting side, the therapist actively organizes a set of tasks that determines the process of therapy. The third dimension is the therapeutic *medium*. At one end, therapy is entirely verbal—just like adult therapy with shorter sentences. At the other, *thematic* play substitutes entirely for direct conversation.

The theoretical landscape is now rich and varied. And, as Cowan (1988) has observed, every theory pairs up with a specific set of targets for intervention. The differences in the practice of child psychotherapy can be traced back toward the particular models of psychopathology held by the therapists. It's possible for theory to direct treatment down a precise road. Some therapists know what strategies they'll use even before they meet a child.

Increasingly, however, developmental and environmental constraints bear heavily on what most of us will end up doing. For example, even if we believe that extended play therapy is most effective for reaching children and resolving internal con-

flicts, it only works if the child is capable of playing symbolically and if the family or insurance company is willing to fund
the endeavor.

After seeing kids for a while, most therapists probably become more "eclectic." Some of the one-to-one connections between theory and practice get a little fuzzy around the edges.
We may treat enuresis in a child, for example, through a combination of parent training, play therapy, and behavioral, cognitive, and client-centered strategies. This increased flexibility is
absolutely an improvement along the way toward treating children as individuals with widely varying needs. *Assessment of the
child's strengths and weaknesses—not theories—should guide the development
of a suitable intervention.* Still, the schools of thought themselves
remain interesting for what they tell us about the many ways we
might view childhood symptoms and the avenues they suggest
for entering a child's world.

No-talk therapy has its roots in many different theoretical
schools, particularly traditional play therapy, client-centered
therapy, and solution-focused approaches. Like traditional child
treatment it emphasizes the healing power of the therapeutic
relationship, but here the focus of the play is different: No-talk
therapy is not necessarily directed toward interpreting symbolic
material, bringing out internalized conflicts, or making sense of
unconscious representations.

Humanistic, client-centered approaches are similarly founded
in empathy and compassion. But they rely much more upon verbal problem-solving, reflecting back to clients in gentle paraphrase what clients describe. By contrast, in no-talk therapy, the
positive regard we have for the child is communicated more in
what we do than in what we say.

Cognitive-behavioral and solution-focused treatments also resemble no-talk therapy, as they highlight strengths and inner
resources, encouraging people to *think* and *act* differently in the
present and the future. But in these approaches, the therapeutic
relationship is of minor interest and really only the precursor to
the real work. Thus, no-talk therapy draws from the interperso-

nal emphases of traditional play therapy and humanist approaches and adds to these the competency-based considerations of the newer cognitive-behavioral and solution-oriented ways of thinking.

But no-talk therapy also goes a pragmatic step beyond traditional methods in three significant ways. First, it embraces developmental and individual differences over other diagnostic considerations. Second, dealing with the child's context—motivations, family, school environment, community—is a major part of the therapy. Finally, the power relationship strives to be overt and egalitarian. Without a reliance on discussing problems, it meets kids on their terms, following their interests and agendas. No-talk therapy is respectful, giving kids the chance to speak for themselves in the ways they are able.

Child Therapists

Interestingly, the theories also have a tremendous amount to say about who *we* are in the therapy room and what is expected of us as therapists. How we behave with kids belies what we predict will work in a given situation. But these frameworks don't just describe the methodology, or therapist's role, but really lead back to our perspective on childhood itself. Do we see kids as a bundle of defenses or behaviors? Do we think that the window to the child's symptoms is through play or language or through work with parents? How much do we reveal of ourselves in the theories we hold most dear? Is there a good match between our personal style with kids and how we think about what ails them? When the treatment is over, how do we measure our degree of success? Given who we are and what we do, are we actually helping kids?

Although there is a notable dearth of research about what makes a child therapist effective, it is probably true that therapists with better "people skills" and the capacity for warmth, empathy, and acceptance are more successful than those who carry a load of problems and preoccupations (e.g., Kazdin, 1991;

Shirk & Saiz, 1992). The little research that exists on therapist factors concludes, not surprisingly, that our own "issues" can indeed adversely affect treatment. For example, preliminary findings indicate that therapists' own attachment histories affect both the levels of interventions they pursue (Dozier, Cue, & Barnett, 1994) and the dropout rates among their clients (Stuart, Pilkonis, Heape, Smith, & Fisher, 1991). These results suggest that our private pasts may show up all too clearly in our treatment of children and adolescents.

Additionally, some of the more interesting speculations about child therapists come from psychoanalytic scholars, who give ample clinical attention to the topic of countertransference. Child treatment arouses in us all kinds of special feelings that stem from our unique childhood experiences and unresolved feelings from the past. Sometimes *we* are speechless as we sort out our own intense and confusing reactions to *them*.

Working with kids, all child therapists, even ones with stunningly good mental health, encounter common dilemmas. The fact that kids are so limited in how they use language (even when they are talking) and behave so unpredictably by adult standards makes child therapy harder for *all* of us. As psychoanalyst Morton Chethik (1989) states so boldly: "Major feelings a child therapist must endure in his work will be *bewilderment* and *complete disorientation*" (italics in original, p. 23) In the course of adult treatment, progress and setbacks follow a fairly predictable path. Seasoned therapists go to work knowing with remarkable certainty what will happen that day. By contrast, we child therapists are frequently totally at sea about why kids behave the way they do. Seemingly out of nowhere they start throwing things around, climbing on furniture, curling into a dejected ball, or getting wildly silly or enraged. Adolescents are almost as inscrutable—sometimes more so. They may jabber on about baroque relationships that require a sociogram to decipher, weep inconsolably, or start clipping their nails onto the floor. And these are the children and teenagers who are *willingly* in the room with us.

The Therapist as Magician

When we agree to see a child or adolescent for therapy, we are entering into an explicit agreement with the referring agent, the parents, the child, and any others with a vested interest in the outcome that we will make a difference, end the problem, and generally "fix the kid." Much like any other specialist, be it a plumber, a dentist, or a tree surgeon, we get paid to change a situation that is causing worry or pain to someone. And, like these other professionals, we have received specialized training and supervision to become competent in the task. But the parallels end there. Leaky faucets, cavities, and dead branches are straightforward problems, and people are usually in agreement about what has happened when the job is done. Child therapy, by contrast, never "fixes" kids—therapists who proclaim they will cure anyone need, as the saying goes, to have *their* heads examined.

Child therapy addresses problems at a particular point in time and in the child's development. As children's cognitive, social, linguistic, and emotional skills evolve, so will their ability to make sense out of confusing and traumatic experiences. Thus, successful therapy may claim to assist a child over a developmental impasse or hurdle, but only so he may go on to the next set of struggles or toward a new comprehension of the old. Such a perspective doesn't imply that troubled kids have to be in therapy multiple times (though quite a few are), but rather that there is no cure for life.

Ultimately, treatment of kids often shares more with the mysterious realms of the unknown than with hard science. We haven't evolved as far as we think in moving from a spiritual to a medical-secular explanation for suffering. And as we help, through the often miraculous wonders of the "therapeutic relationship," we can't say concretely what it is we have *done*. This gift of healing often enables us to buy into our own narcissistic need to deliver all that is expected of us. But it is hard to retain both a passionate belief in our ability to help and a profound humility about the limits of what we can offer.

While all therapists need to struggle against being viewed as having special powers, the problem is more acute for child therapists. Certainly, the treatment of adults can be hazardous because therapeutic "reparenting" can create unnecessary regression, making dependent children out of them. In the 1970s, Thomas Szasz raised concerns about the power imbalance of traditional therapy (Szasz, 1974). He saw the paternalistic parallel between therapy with needy clients and the parenting of needy children. Indeed, traditional therapies that require us to appear wise and mysterious may perpetuate the humorous notion that we have aces up our sleeves and can read minds.

But child therapists have an even more complicated set of roles and expectations. By treating kids who are not themselves requesting therapy, or are developmentally incapable of doing so, we are entering a gray area filled with competing and conflicting hopes, fears, and expectations. This ambiguity is most evident in cases of child abuse, where we often work to keep or reunite kids with parents who have harmed or neglected them. But these parents, too, have their own developmental limitations. Some parents only get help for themselves *through* their kids. In some cases, we are also potentially parenting the *parents*. Although we usually have an "identified patient," we seldom have just one family member in our care. And since the children are still dependent, we are engaged in a kind of simultaneous "reparenting" alongside the actual parents, sometimes supporting, sometimes contradicting the parent's style and methods.

At some point along the way, the parents' needs for us to "do something" and the child's exquisite vulnerability can work together to mobilize our own hubris, leading to grandiose—and magical—plans for treatment. Our shame and disappointment when we doubt ourselves or sense insufficient progress can be devastating reminders of the size of these expectations. Learning that a parent or colleague is skeptical of our work further erodes our lofty hopes. But none of these external wrecking balls is as effective as a no-talk kid defying us to do something helpful—or even vaguely interesting. As one such child commented politely part way through a long first hour, "No offense or anything, but this is a complete waste of time."

Guarding against a belief in our magical powers does not mean we should also defend against magical moments in therapy. But these may only occur when we become willing to put our wands and potions aside and agree to get to know a child on her own terms. This may mean *expressing* self-doubt, curiosity, amazement, and bewilderment. Our willingness to come out—on our own—from behind the Wizard's curtain creates the room for change and other possibilities.

The Therapist as Policeman

Another set of expectations for therapy tends to come out of such oddly disparate places as courts, structural family therapy, the Christian Coalition, and Toughlove, among others. These strange bedfellows have in common the hierarchical belief that children and adolescents do better when adults are in control. When acting-out kids are sent to therapy, referring sources typically believe (often accurately) that the kids are running the show at home. This frequently translates into a request for the therapist to assist the parents in reasserting their wavering or lost authority. While the expectation can have some magical subtexts, the therapist in these cases may primarily function as a policeman, establishing firm consequences and assisting the parents in follow-through. With children of single mothers, or kids who are being under-parented, we are asked to step in as something more than another parent—as a kind of big brother to whom infractions are reported weekly, and who will closely monitor both the child and the progress.

While this authoritarian role is clearest in court-ordered therapy cases, many other kids feel that being forced into treatment is tantamount to a court order. In either situation, adult wishes may have been presented, over a period of time, in a coercive and punitive manner. Concerned adults see the child as someone who needs to know "who is boss." Therapy is sometimes the ultimate threat in a series of "Do this or else" strategies to create a more compliant kid. It can be quite discouraging to discover that attending therapy appears on the same list as grounding, losing recess, or calling the police.

The hope for our magic usually comes from people who see a child's *troubled* behavior as a reflection of emotional pain. The hope for our policing more typically arises when referring agents view a child's *troubling* behavior as a violation of family or community standards. In fact, the events precipitating either sort of referral can be entirely the same. What distinguishes the routes into therapy, and thus the expectation for our involvement, is often better explained by prejudices of race, class, gender and culture.

SICK KIDS AND BAD KIDS

No-talk kids are typically referred through these two distinct conduits. The first, the "sick kids," are often middle-class and white. If outpatient therapy doesn't ameliorate the problem, they are apt to be sent for a psychiatric hospitalization or therapeutic residential treatment. Girls, whose acting-out behaviors may wind up hurting *them* (e.g., sex, drugs, running away), get treatment as a rule (as opposed to juvenile justice). Non-minority boys are also more likely to be given the benefit of the doubt and to be routed through the mental health system. Even if they engage in delinquent or predelinquent activities like shoplifting, vandalism, truancy, or fighting, their underlying problems are still the focus.

The second group of referrals arrives through the juvenile-justice system or another disciplinary channel. These are the "bad kids" who are sent into therapy out of a primary concern for family or community safety. The child, usually (though not always) an impoverished or minority kid, is acting in such a way as to make adults angry as well as concerned. Therapy is often part of a list of restrictive expectations that may also include community service, adhering to a curfew, and checking in with someone associated with the court, like a probation officer.

Treatment then becomes part of the web of services deemed necessary by adults to prevent out-of-home placement. Parents may want desperately to regain their authority, and some will work tenaciously to keep custody of their kids. Many times, though, they are burdened by their own difficulties—poverty, substance use, violence, histories of abuse—and are well on their way to giving up. They can't invest much in their children, or, as an extension, in family therapy. No-talk kids without committed parents are at the greatest risk of all. They'll need a tight and determined circle of adults around them even to approximate providing all they have lost.

Our purpose will differ if we work as part of a sick kid's or a bad kid's team. Even if we disagree mightily with the frame offered to us, we still need to see how it operates in the lives of our young clients. And even if we view ourselves as therapy's version of Dennis Rodman—basketball's athletically gifted but socially divergent renegade—and want to play according to our own rules, we must still acknowledge (as he does) the roles and functions of the rest of the team. For example, a teenager referred as part of a diversion program in juvenile or family court usually knows that the court will be receiving progress reports and telephone exchanges about him. Even as we try to win him over with a careful articulation of the principles of confidentiality and our own supportive belief about what has gotten him to this point, he may continue to see us, with good reason, as another untrustworthy agent of the court.

Similarly, if our "team" includes overwhelming or abusive parents, loathed school principals, powerful child protection workers, or intimidating doctors, we'll face an uphill battle attempting to distinguish ourselves from the rest of the pack. We may be able to see all the ways we are different from "them," but, in reality, we are more alike than we think. The very fact of our adulthood is sufficient evidence of that.

The dilemma here is that all kids—and especially no-talk kids—need this circle of adults around them who are invested in their well-being. However, if the circle feels more like a choke than an embrace, therapy becomes just one more strangling link. Our vision of our purpose must also include an understanding of both how the child or adolescent sees us and how we fit into this larger circle.

The potential for the therapeutic relationship—with sick kids *and* bad kids—increases considerably with the circle around us too. First, the circle lessens the pressure on us to be the Wizard and allows us instead to do the things we do best—listen, play, feel, connect. Second, it enables us to participate as a part of the child's actual life instead of being some sort of extraterrestrial experience that is without context. Third, we can help the circle become bigger and stronger. Rather than assuming the entire treatment function for the child, we can imagine the team including players from every aspect of the child's life. Perhaps most importantly, we can renegotiate our role on the team if it is not compatible with what we feel is most needed. If the referral calls for a magician or a policeman, we can redefine who we are as part of the circle and not feel compelled to shoulder the entire problem. The circle doesn't just help us do our jobs better—though that's reason enough to have one around a child or adolescent. Kids are often profoundly moved to walk into a room filled with people who care about them. At times, identifying and convening a circle of adults can be the best intervention of all.

6

Fun, Food, and Flexibility

THE NO-TALK THERAPIST shares many characteristics of all child
and adolescent therapists—interest in development, a willingness to play games, tolerance of chaos—but in no-talk therapy,
these become more overt, even exaggerated. We are hyper-con-
scious of how we see ourselves and our roles, and of how we
want to be viewed by no-talk kids. Since the therapeutic relationship is often our focus, the way we "show up" in the treatment is of central importance.

CHARACTERISTICS OF THE NO-TALK THERAPIST

The no-talk therapist also needs to develop other qualities that
are entirely unconventional. Meeting kids on their own terms is
difficult for most adults and, in ways, the better our training, the
harder this leap to divergent thought. But the no-talk wall is
often scaled only by someone willing to be absurdly creative.
And any generalizations about what makes a "good" no-talk therapist must be tempered with respect for each person's individual
style; we can't all be Carl Whitaker.

Liking Kids

Although it may seem obvious, it is vital that we like the particular child or adolescent we are planning to treat. We don't have to like everything about her or maintain this high esteem all the time, but we need to be able to keep some kind of genuine positive regard in our minds throughout the therapy.

It's more difficult to like no-talk kids; there's no doubt about it. They tend to progress more slowly and with significantly less gratitude than other children. They resist the relationship and can be devastatingly rejecting. And they can press our buttons, every one of them. A teenager may scrutinize our every flaw with the same attention he applies to examining his acne in the mirror. Any affection we are able to generate may be fragile, easily undermined by professional burn-out, problems with payment, a lopsided caseload with too many difficult kids, or personal troubles of our own. But without affection there can be no therapy. Kids for whom we feel only obligation or repulsion need to be referred elsewhere.

No-talk therapy has fewer techniques to hide behind; the therapist must place more emphasis on being three-dimensional. So the process of liking a kid can also become the stuff of the treatment. Sometimes we must slog through the mud of our own reactions, sifting out old impatiences and inadequacies that catch our boots, so we can attend more effectively to what we like about a particular child or adolescent.

Personal Childhood Memories

More than other approaches, no-talk therapy requires that we be in touch with the more childlike parts of ourselves. Having no memories of our own lives before age 12 bodes poorly for our effectiveness with no-talk kids. Since our level of empathy must remain unusually high, we need to recall as much as possible about what it felt like being a kid. We don't need to have had *Leave It to Beaver* childhoods, but we do need to be able to have within us some of the mix of experiences that growing up brings.

This is not to suggest that no-talk therapists are Peter Pans, stuck at some earlier developmental stage; we must always function as integrated adults with these kids. But our memories guide us more than we may realize. For example, most of us can recall engaging in some task alongside our parents, when conversation was not the principal means of communication. We may remember washing and drying dishes, driving in the car, going fishing, raking leaves, folding laundry, singing or playing catch. Many intimate family moments probably lacked focused dialogue. How those times felt, how they developed, and who we were can guide us down the no-talk path.

Our own painful stories can also serve as a beacon. Our troubles growing up connect us to the alienated or injured no-talk kid. We need to be aware, at some level, of how rejection, disappointment, confusion, and loss felt to us when we were six or 10 or 15. We don't need to tell them about it, of course, but by holding this experience gently within ourselves we can assist them in cradling their own hurts.

Our memories of school can be particularly informative. Recollections about what made teachers special to us, what we liked most and least about different classes, and how our contact with adults there had an impact on us can provide important information about the roles of adults in these kids' lives. For example, we may remember favorite teachers with a vivid tenderness that can be quite telling. We might say that these teachers were firm but fair, or appreciative of individual differences, that they had a good sense of humor, cared, made kids feel special, and seemed to really enjoy their work. As we review these qualities, we realize that they are not much different, at least on the face of things, from what can make therapists memorable, too.

Enthusiasm

No-talk therapists need to be capable of cheerleader-type enthusiasm, whether or not it's expressed at such a fevered pitch. There are times that are appropriate for all varieties of pom-pom waving. Many kids we treat, for example, have not had the pleasure of seeing their paintings on the fridge or the wall at home. That simple gesture of enthusiasm is relatively quiet, but contains wonderful affirmation. Sometimes the display of artwork or a few words of praise are all the no-talk kid can tolerate, anyway.

Our enthusiasm has to be respectful and genuine; kids know and hate condescension and effusive, unjustified praise. Enthusiasm can be implied rather than spoken. We also demonstrate it when we visit their classrooms or get beaten at Crazy Eights. For some kids we also need to be unabashed about giving high-fives, applause, and cheers. If positive regard were air travel, no-talk enthusiasm would be first-class treatment.

Enthusiasm is also about being able to act like a child and becoming excited about the things children enjoy. Sometimes it is hard to be on the wavelength of a kid who is interested only in listening to the lyrics of a Nirvana CD or smashing dinosaurs into each other, but it is worth the extra effort it takes to decipher what Cobain is saying or to make a Stegosaurus roar. And it's probably good to discover we can tolerate such regression in ourselves; being an adult all of the time has its limitations. Of course, it is easier when kids are excited about things we once enjoyed, because, knowing what it is, we can return seamlessly to that pleasure. For better or worse, Legos and the Grateful Dead have both been around for a couple of generations now. But even when the passions are alien to us the *feeling* of childlike excitement must still be available for no-talk therapy to succeed.

Warmth

No-talk therapists are nice people. We work at leaving our sharp edges and cynicism at home. By the "gleam in our eyes," kids know we're ready to make a connection with them on their terms. From the decor of our offices to the way we dress and talk, kids know. The warmth we radiate sends real messages: *She likes me, therefore I am likable. I give her pleasure and I help her, therefore I am worthwhile. She knows about my behavior and still wants to play with me, therefore I am good enough.*

Of course, all kid therapists need to be kind and respectful. But again, in no-talk therapy this quality has to shine through consciously and steadily. These kids will work very hard to put out the fire and to turn our gleams into glowers. Although it doesn't have to be, their silence is frequently cold and scornful, like an icy wall between us. Our even warmth over time can melt away this barrier.

Imperfection

One of the benefits—for us—of this kind of treatment is the inherent virtue of therapist imperfection. No-talk kids are so well-versed in screwing up that they delight in seeing they are not alone. With adult clients, it is important to look put-together, have a tidy office, and run a tight schedule. Even with more traditional child therapy, we try to conceal our personality quirks and flaws as best we can. But here everything everyone brings into the room is grist for the mill.

This is not to suggest that we have to run 20 minutes late and wear mismatched socks, or pile our desks to overflowing and spill paint on the furniture. But should such irregularities occur, we can turn them to good use. For example, our own struggles keeping "a clean room" may resonate deeply with the young adolescent. Similarly, our deficits doing things according to schedule may strike a familiar chord with a kid who has trouble handing in assignments on time or making a curfew.

Parental Instincts

One of the great unresolved questions of child therapy is whether kids are better served by therapists who are parents in real life. This debate has echoes in other fields of treatment; some people say only recovered addicts can treat drug abusers effectively. But while it does seem likely that parents may more readily heed advice from someone "who really knows what it is like," most kids don't know the difference. It is true that our approach to child therapy, our sense of norms, frustrations, and concerns, shifts after we have kids of our own. But all kid therapists can develop "parental instincts," whether or not they get to practice after hours.

These "instincts" may include, for example, a desire to protect kids from danger, a distinct pleasure in their accomplishments, and an immediate anguished reaction on hearing of their pain. Without ever replacing the broad and complex functions of actual parents, no-talk therapists need to develop these nurturing responses to kids. In fact, it is sometimes easier to have such "instincts" when the troubled or troubling child is not our own. This greater distance enables us to remain utterly concerned while relieving us of the additional burdens of having to attend Thanksgiving dinner with the 16-year-old fasting vegetarian anarchists we are treating.

Frustration Tolerance

One of the hallmarks of no-talk kids is their low tolerance of frustration. They are highly reactive to their environments and can be set off by seemingly minor disruptions in routine or difficulty completing a trivial task. Their solutions reflect both their deficits in coping skills and their sense that adults are unhelpful. By withdrawing from discussion, they set an obstacle course for us to get through. This may give us a marvelous window into their feelings of hopelessness, but at the same time it sets *us* up to be unbearably frustrated.

These kids are hard. They usually come from families that are hard. They probably live in environments that are hard. They often have insurance policies that are hard. Accordingly, by the time they come to therapy, things may have calcified all the way around. This work requires that we develop unusually *high* frustration tolerance. A no-talk therapist needs to be patient and can't take it too personally when a kid tells her she's a "useless jerk" (to phrase it euphemistically).

Silence in therapy can be uncomfortable. In fact, most of us would prefer a good fight to "the silent treatment." And many kids acknowledge they'd rather adults yelled at them than ignored them. So we may all feel that not talking in therapy is the ultimate weapon. As therapists we may be hurt, angry, and frustrated because of our expectation that kids will like us and talk to us as we imagine they should. We need to remember that these kids are managing their lives the only way they know how. We should *expect* to be frustrated, as a matter of course, and to forge onward anyway.

Flexibility and Creativity

Michael Jordan is an extraordinary basketball player because he can, in midair, change hands, direction, plans, and the course of the game. He can jump up and achieve what few of us can manage even firmly planted. When he gets the ball he uses the activity on the floor, at that moment, to tell him what to try next. (And he looks good doing it!)

No-talk therapists aspire to be to child treatment what Michael Jordan is to basketball—and even mere mortals *can* succeed. The ordinary tendency in therapy, as in life, is quite the opposite—to decide what to do and then keep doing more of it, regardless of outcome. Married couples have the same fights in the same way for 40 years. Parents put kids in time-out for longer durations even though time-out has *never* worked for them. People diet, date, and dream in repetitive and evidently unproductive ways, with a compulsive zeal that is heroic only in its futility.

Imagine, instead, therapy without expectations. Having only the bare outlines of various game-plans, we wait to see and sense what might work next. All sorts of moves are possible. We can try something different in a flash, sit silently, act frantically, intervene decisively, change directions, turn the time around. We can build a tower to the ceiling, gamble for pennies, make pudding, take a walk, sit in a tent, do a magic trick, write a secret code, arm wrestle, invent a board game, play on the computer,

or even play basketball, so we really can "be like Mike." The
point here is that it is human nature to become anxious and rigid
when we have a set idea that doesn't get followed; our tendency
is to try harder at more of the same. No-talk therapy can be
liberating precisely because it has so few expectations to disap-
point us.

Touch

Many traditionally trained child therapists are careful to define
their personal boundaries. Some even hesitate to leave their
chairs and do all their work with kids from a safe distance in the
room. This rule of noncontact is supported by contemporary
trends in therapy litigation that lead us to believe we *can't* be too
careful. And for abused kids, who have all kinds of difficulties
managing their physical space, we *do* have to be respectful and
clear. In some cases, we'll have to limit a child's indiscriminate
and overwhelming need to touch us, providing boundaries and
modeling more acceptable ways of establishing contact. In
others, we'll need to maintain a careful distance, knowing that
any touch may be misinterpreted by the child as a sexual advance or a physical threat.

For male therapists, decisions about touching are tougher to
make. At this time in our culture it's easier for a woman to hug a
child. But children, especially boys, need safe touching from
men, too, and actively seek it out. People may expect that little
girls want to sit on laps and cuddle; generally, we stop encouraging boys to have physical contact at an earlier age. It's a shame
that men have to feel more self-conscious in this litigious age.
Kids often crave the contact, and it *can* be a healthy part of no-
talk therapy.

Rigid rules about touch make no sense in no-talk therapy,
especially with younger kids. Of course, since we follow their
leads, we won't initiate much more than a pat on the back or a
high-five on our own. But if a kid wants a goodbye hug at the
end of an enjoyable hour, we certainly indulge it. Preadolescents

often have a genuine need for physical affection and will feel hurt and alienated if their overtures are rebuked. Furthermore, as part of their own healing, these kids often have to learn how to ask for, and to say no to, physical contact. Our physical connection may provide them with safe practice in good touching.

In the course of therapy, kids may lean against us doing a project, run into our arms when they see us, and hold our hands going places. For some, the most therapeutic intervention we can offer is a snuggle on the couch with a good book! Touch can be a valuable part of no-talk therapy, when offered with respect and true affection. While adolescents pose greater concerns here, because they are more apt to sexualize meaning, we still need to be open to the possibility that, in some cases, a squeeze of a shoulder on the way out the door, or even a farewell hug, can be entirely therapeutic and validating.

The guidelines for touch in therapy with kids are these: Physical contact should obviously never be sexualized. It must serve a therapeutic purpose to build upon a safe and caring relationship. It should be offered empathically, to a particular child at a particular time, and not just as a routine part of practice. Kids should initiate any contact that goes beyond a tap on the back or arm or a handshake. Physical restraint should be used as a very last resort. Parents need to be told in advance that we may use particular kinds of touch in therapy, and we should specify with them what these are. We need to use touch naturally, as an authentic extension of who we really are in this relationship.

Fun

Richard Gardner (1975) talks about three forms of reasoning required for working with kids. In addition to inductive and deductive reasoning, Gardner suggests, we also need to include "seductive reasoning." By this he means thinking about how to join with a child on his own terms. This isn't hard to comprehend: Kids just wanna have fun.

The business of psychotherapy is becoming increasingly

stuffy. Our journals and meetings, with few exceptions, are ever more grown-up and dull. The hours we crank out, with our thoughtful goals and objectives, our adultified dialogues, and our behavioral charts, are just as boring. Caught in the belief that therapy can turn into actual science if we try hard enough, we mistakenly think that we're supposed to be *working* with kids to help them. Freeman et al. (1997) voice a similar complaint:

> Problems tend to be grim. If they had a credo, it might well be: "Take us seriously!" After all, serious problems demand to be taken this way, do they not? To the degree that a problem is oppressive, the gravity of our attention and the severity of measures taken to remedy it seem bound to increase. Inviting worry, despair, and hopelessness, weighty problems can immobilize families as well as the people who serve them. We wonder whether it is to the problems' advantage to be taken quite so seriously. By the same token, is their very existence threatened by humor and playfulness? (p. 3)

As a vital component to no-talk therapy, fun deserves respect as an intervention, as worthy as any other. Of course, it is simply impossible to order someone to "have a sense of humor" or "be funny." Still, the therapists who are successful with no-talk kids generally have a light touch; we're generous with witticisms and irony, incredulity and amusement, willing to see the absurdity of a position or a situation and able to laugh at ourselves, too.

Food

No-talk therapists feed clients. Food is important for kids, even beyond the obvious and seminal links it has to nurturance. Since children and adolescents are still growing, they mostly need to graze a bit throughout the day; this is another quality that separates them from adults. In fact, for some kids, managing their blood sugar may be the secret to success, and enough well-timed carbs can prevent a good percentage of melt-downs. But, even in less extreme situations, it is fairly pointless—and not very kind—to try to delve into the emotional world of a hungry kid.

Feeding kids in therapy is controversial. Some therapists (who believe that the nurturance should be symbolic and not real) would not dream of providing snacks for their clients. But because our approach is pragmatic, it's okay for no-talk kids to eat in therapy if they want to. In reality, when we see them after school most kids won't have eaten for several hours, assuming they even had lunch. Sometimes they know they are hungry and will say so. At other times, they will just be crabby and frustrated.

Proper nutrition also has irrefutable health and mental health benefits. Making nutritious snacks provides an ideal opportunity for future discussions about how we take care of ourselves. Therapeutic snacking demonstrates both the symbolic and real kinds of "feeding" that people do; relationships can be nourishing in many ways.

Food preparation is also a great side-by-side activity, and one that ends with a satisfying conclusion. The advent of the microwave in most offices has opened up an even greater range of "cooking" possibilities. Cookbooks for kids may provide additional suggestions for the ambitious and interested chef-therapist. But even simple snacks like soup, English muffin pizza, pudding, ants-on-a-log, peanut butter on crackers, or fruit smoothies can be therapeutic to prepare and enjoyable to consume.

Cool Stuff

No-talk therapists have lots of "cool stuff" to do—props and activities at the ready. The office needs to look inviting, and we want to be able to generate a little enthusiasm for our set-up from the beginning. We need to suit our ideas to the chronological and developmental levels of the kids, and it's better to err on the too-young side. Thus, if a 10-year-old appears interested in assembling a model car, we might begin with a snap-together kit before venturing into the complex area of tiny pieces and smelly glue. Similarly, easier puzzles, recipes, games, or constructions should precede more difficult ones. It also helps to have some gorgeous materials casually draped around the room to get the no-talk juices flowing.

Advocacy

No-talk therapists do more than treat kids; we advocate for them, too. In individual therapy we work hard to let them know we are on their team. We make a commitment to their safety, to their empowerment, to fun. Advocacy, not surprisingly at this most essential point, aims to give them a voice with us.

In family negotiations, we are not just impartial mediators, as in more traditional practice. We need to be willing to take sides, seeing the disagreement from the child's perspective. As we help no-talk kids negotiate and stand up for themselves in a more effective way, our advocacy can return to the cheering sidelines. But during the crises and struggles that invariably erupt with no-talk kids and their parents, our advocacy must be vocal and apparent. We may warn parents ahead of time that we will be siding with their child to help her develop a coherent position, so they aren't surprised when we emphatically play favorites in family sessions.

Our advocacy role continues in school, to ensure that the child gets the supports she needs. We help parents meet with school teachers and administrators to arrange particular services (e.g., tutoring, an Individualized Education Plan, after-school activities, or a social-skills group). We remain involved with schools from year to year as necessary, bringing other adults into the circle and critical interventions into place.

Our community advocacy role includes knowing what is available for kids and families—places where they can have some success, meet other kids, and have a good time. A big part of our advocacy is devoted to forming bridges to new and positive experiences outside of school and therapy. If the children and adolescents we see get into after-school programs that can't handle their behavior, we take our bag of tricks on the road and consult with the staff about what else they might try. In community advocacy, we become collaborators, helping to coordinate services among the different professionals and agencies.

Empathy Galore

No-talk kids need a relationship with someone who thinks they are marvelous. Urie Bronfenbrenner effectively described the no-talk therapist when he wrote, "In order to develop normally, a child needs the enduring, irrational involvement of one or more adults in care and joint activity with that child. . . . In short, someone has to be crazy about that kid" (Bronfenbrenner & Weiss, 1983, p. 398). The therapeutic relationship exceeds admiration by calling upon a deep reservoir of empathy.

When we become truly empathic, we can understand and feel what is most important to children or adolescents. We want to be able to see the world—and ourselves—through *their* eyes. We can focus our concern by considering tough questions:

- If she drew a picture of me, what would it look like?
- If he described me to his friends, what would he say?
- If she wrote me a letter, what would she write?
- If he wrote a letter to his parents about therapy, what would he write?
- How far apart are we: What is the difference between how I see myself and how he sees me?
- If she talked to me, what do I think she would tell me?
- Do I like this kid?
- Do I like myself when I'm with him?
- How much realistic hope can I generate about him and his life?
- Why isn't she talking to me in therapy? Is this a reason I completely understand?
- If I were he, would I do exactly as he does?
- What does it feel like for her, coming to see me at this time under these circumstances?

- How much difference is there between what I think is in this child's best interests and what *he* wants for his own life?
- What *does* she care about?

These kinds of questions get us out of our own heads and into theirs. The new perspective, in turn, moves us to act less like a magician or a policeman and more like someone who cares.

But *feeling* empathic is insufficient—clearly, we also have to communicate it to the child or adolescent who comes to therapy with his particular social map, including a painful history and a variety of symptoms. Whether or not he talks about his situation, he communicates something about himself simply by the way he enters the room. Usually there is some kind of expression as well, even if it is a scowl or a muttered complaint that he would prefer to be somewhere else. We must then respond, indicating we "get it." Our reaction can be verbal, but it is often better communicated some other way—through play or gesture, or even through shifting gears altogether—moving the child out of the hot seat and into our cool stuff.

We manifest empathy to the child or adolescent through our willingness to try something different, something that is less shaming and oppressive than talking about feelings. One of the consequences is that kids may then begin the long journey toward being more empathic toward themselves. Daniel Stern (1985) has talked about the process of "attunement" between parent and infant, whereby successful parents become increasingly responsive to the needs and rhythms of their babies. This attunement shapes the relationship in a reciprocal fashion, with a kind of feedback loop developing in both parties. A parent's sensitivity to the unique wiring and developmental level of her infant is much like the empathic responsiveness of a no-talk therapist. We also fine-tune our sensitivity over time as patterns become familiar.

The Zen Way

Like kids and Zen masters, good no-talk therapists can get into the present moment, not worrying about what happens next or evaluating each move as it is made. It's too bad that we're trained in the scientific method; it often impedes our ability to make connections with kids. Instead, it's often helpful in no-talk therapy to be relaxed, alert, and in the present, aware only of what it is like being with this particular child in this passing moment, not needing anyone to do more. Sometimes the silence is actually the peaceful absence of noise and bickering—if we can stop strategizing and just accept it.

Consultation

Because no-talk therapy is a humbling kind of experience, it should be no surprise that no-talk therapists are not too proud to engage in all kinds of professional consultation. The primary consultants are, of course, the no-talk kids themselves. Frequently, we seek their counsel about how we might help them, and even ask their advice about what they recommend to help other kids we know.

The circle of adults can provide ad hoc consultants, too. We may collaborate in therapeutic goal-setting to ensure that all involved have the same priorities. For example, a young adolescent in academic trouble may have as a primary goal not flunking out of school. Therapy, tutoring and a range of other supports should all share this objective. Sometimes we don't know what the best agenda is—the no-talk kid has so many deficits that it's hard to focus on one or two. The team can then help us pick a direction for treatment. Such consultation can provide realistic and consistent support to the child.

As professionals, we tend to seek consultation from like-minded professionals. Typically, psychologists talk to psychologists, social workers to social workers, school counselors to school counselors. Although we can learn a great deal from our peers, we remain in a ghetto of ideas when we do this and may be quite astonished to learn about wonderful ways for reaching no-talk kids that others have come up with, outside of our particular field of expertise. For example, I learned from a scoutmaster that one silent 11-year-old boy was quite chatty inside a tent. The next week, I borrowed a little tent and brought it to work. The child taught me how to set it up, right in my office, and for the whole hour we sat cozily inside, telling ghost stories to each other. With these kids, we need to be tenacious about hunting down new approaches.

In addition to the usual peer supervision outside the therapy room, it can be helpful to stage such a supervision in front of the no-talk kid. In this consultation, the therapist and another professional discuss the dilemmas of treatment in front of the child or adolescent, and the therapist admits to needing help. Sometimes a no-talk kid who has been unwilling to talk about much of anything will happily discuss the shortcomings of her therapist with the consultant! Such an intervention can be powerful and transformative, encouraging a child or adolescent to take greater ownership of the therapy, as well as providing the therapist with unexpected leads and insights.

Consultation can also expand the child's sense of having more resources than just the therapist. For example, going to another therapist's office for a Lego consultation or a knock-knock joke demonstrates that other adults out there can also help. Kids are also entitled to a consultation when they disagree with their therapist—about the rules of a game, for example. Consultation expands the circle around the child for information as well as support.

In no-talk therapy, we may end up following children and adolescents to places we haven't traveled before, which are frequently not on the itinerary of the referring adults. We follow the lead of kids who have never been in front before. And in preserving the integrity of no-talk kids we do much to foster our own.

7

No-Talk Diagnosis and Assessment

THERAPY WITH NO-TALK kids proceeds (like life) from the center out, not the reverse. There are many combinations of reasons and histories that lead a child or adolescent away from deep conversation with a therapist. Until we have a firm grasp of the core meaning of the silence, we will not be helpful. The initial weeks of therapy may contain the seeds for later work, but our primary focus needs to remain on the therapeutic relationship. Our essential task is joining the no-talk kid on her unique developmental runway.

ASSESSMENT AND UNDERSTANDING

As with most types of child therapy, assessment may include a variety of methods. It really depends upon how impenetrable and mysterious the silence is. Assessment strategies may include, for example, family sessions, school observations, playing games, psychological testing, conversations with friends and relatives, creating and meeting with a circle of adults, drawing up a contract with the no-talk kid, and detailing a developmental history. Data collection should evolve from different angles and sources. It needs to include enough information to get a sense of what makes the particular child or adolescent tick—his strengths and weaknesses—and an idea of a way in. Only then we can proceed to build a therapy together.

Differential diagnosis in no-talk therapy is not quite the same as in traditional medical-model approaches. We don't rule out diagnoses but remain open to all possible considerations in a dynamic, ongoing way. Because complex kids can have multiple and interrelated diagnoses, we need to stay thoughtful and planful even after the assessment period is over. For example, many traumatized kids appear to have attention deficits as well. Some of these kids need to be treated for trauma-related problems, and then they become less distractible. Others appear to have both problems. As we decide what to treat, we need to remain aware of other areas of concern.

The most important aspect of assessment is how it leads us toward the best intervention. Kids are like Hansel and Gretel, leaving trail markers along their path to silence. Once we recognize the breadcrumbs, we know we're headed in the right direction. Of course, thorough assessment also leads to accurate diagnosis. But just relying on diagnosis is like knowing Hansel and Gretel are in the woods but having no clue about what trail to follow to reach them.

For example, no-talk kids frequently meet criteria for oppositional-defiant disorder. Their propensity for limit-testing can stem from biological and genetic conditions, child abuse, attention, language, and learning deficits, inconsistent parenting, depression, drug abuse, seizures, psychosis, involvement with a marginal peer group, inadequate social problem-solving skills, or some combination of these difficulties. Each of these explanations leads to its own set of treatment goals. Thus, the label of ODD is insufficient—and interesting only as it leads us to ask questions about the origins of the problem. *In no-talk therapy, our explanation for the problem guides the intervention.* While still important to consider, the diagnosis is usually less helpful.

The Developmental Deficits Model

All no-talk kids have deficits that make the requirements of traditional therapy overwhelming for them. For example, instead of viewing an oppositional-defiant kid as a troublemaker, out to violate rules and expectations, we might see the behavior as the result of a major deficit in social skills (Greene, 1998) or in emotional regulation. The child or adolescent may not have learned more adaptive social problem-solving. She may have a learning disability, with delays in frustration tolerance, in empathic thinking, in self-soothing. Or she may have the necessary skills and a performance deficit when it comes to stressful situations. Put in this developmental perspective, many of the behaviors descriptive of ODD are quite typical for two- or three-year-olds. In the face of a particular developmental delay or "learning disability," our treatment strategies become more focused and clear.

The evaluation and treatment of developmental deficits typically follow two parallel and essential tracks. These include delineating the areas of delay and fostering competencies. Both approaches are essential to no-talk therapy—with relatively more focus on areas of proficiency during the assessment period.

Diagnosis of No-Talk Kids

No-talk kids are harder to diagnose for several reasons. Most obviously, it is tough to make an accurate diagnosis of someone who isn't communicating productively. Also, as mentioned, these kids tend to have interrelated problems that meet criteria for several concurrent diagnoses. Further, their unwillingness or inability to form new relationships compounds many symptoms, exacerbating old deficits and making the ground fertile for new ones. In the absence of thoughtful conversation, verbal problem-solving, connections with others, and new learning, a child's difficulties become deeper and more extensive.

We usually find out about kids by asking them for their stories and making sense of the quality and content of their responses. When this avenue for information isn't available, we must turn to their silence—also an important pathway into how they may be feeling. In the classical sense, when children refuse to talk or play in any way that means exposure, risk, or engagement with the therapist, they are resisting therapy. But no-talk kids are doing more than just resisting; they have important reasons for being unable or unwilling to communicate in expected ways.

COMMON DIAGNOSIS OF NO-TALK KIDS

Among the most common reasons kids don't talk in therapy are a lack verbal and social skills, boredom, opposition for its own sake or for power, feeling trapped, disengagement, and shyness. Each may be associated with a variety of diagnoses, environmental variables, and referral questions. When a no-talk kid winds up in a therapist's office, it's essential to know both the story that got him there and how that story has led to silence. All of the information we gather will bear heavily on therapeutic decisions that follow.

Lack of Skill

Colin is a seven-year-old foster child with a significant history of neglect, trauma, multiple placements, developmental delays, and some hearing loss, particularly in one ear. His play is rigid and repetitive: He stacks Legos to look like primitive airplanes, then waves them around making engine noises, or lines up matchbox cars carefully, for the entire hour. Colin doesn't know how to play with someone else, and his isolation seems defensive—he doesn't want to let anyone in. He also has substantial language deficits in both comprehension and expression that further limit his ability to engage with me.

Colin's foster parents, who are considering adoption, would like him to be able to feel and behave better. At home, in rages that erupt for seemingly minor frustrations and transitions, he has broken windows and harmed himself and others. Colin doesn't talk easily, as might be expected. He has an unusually long reaction time when spoken to, even when he hears information that is interesting to him. He seems to ignore any and all questions about how things are going, and he dissociates under stress. Thus, when Colin doesn't respond in therapy, it is possible he hasn't heard the question, is ignoring it, or is dissociating.

For traditional treatment to be successful with Colin, he'd have to gain a window into how he is feeling, identify triggers to different emotional states, match feelings to behaviors—and how people have responded to him—and sort out what to do next. This is an extremely difficult task for Colin, made even more so because he is probably flooded with several emotions. It is very likely, for example, that he is mad, sad, worried, scared, and hopeful in his new foster home. Which feeling should he be in touch with when he breaks a window there? Some delayed children like Colin can develop sufficient skills to manage a more usual course of treatment. But many do not, and like all kids with a lack of "therapy skills" they can be helped in the interim.

Diagnosis
Colin easily met criteria for several diagnoses: His struggles could best be explained by a combination of learning disabilities, ADHD, attachment disorder, PTSD, and perhaps more a specific anxiety disorder as well. The symptoms of attachment disorder and PTSD were predominant, however, and became the primary focus of his treatment.

Many children sent to therapy lack the skills necessary to talk or play in meaningful ways. Like Colin, they may have attachment difficulties, a history of severe abuse and neglect, or other kinds of cognitive and social deficits. A relatively high level of play, language, and social skills is required for success in traditional therapy. Yet it is precisely because of deficits in these areas that children are referred for treatment in the first place. Young children who don't play thematically, as well as older children and adolescents who cannot manage the verbal tasks of active problem-solving, are simply not able to explore their inner worlds in any meaningful way. No-talk kids who lack "therapy skills" may meet the criteria for one or more of the following diagnoses:

- Mental retardation
- Learning disabilities
- Attention deficit hyperactivity disorder
- Pervasive developmental disorder
- Receptive and/or expressive language disorder
- Reactive attachment disorder of early childhood
- Post-traumatic stress disorder
- Anxiety or depressive disorder

Boredom

Betsy is a 12-year-old girl who is generally managing most of the tasks of early adolescence adequately. Both of her parents have histories of depression and alcohol use, and they are being treated with antidepressants, 12-step programs, and therapy. When Betsy's mother found morbid poetry in her room and, later that week, saw her weeping over social struggles at school, she thought she saw a familiar depressive style emerging. Desperately wanting to protect Betsy from repeating the family pattern, she brought her child, unwillingly, to therapy.

Betsy was quick to note that her mother had overreacted and before long added, "Not everyone thinks therapy is interesting." She rejected the notion that having someone to talk to would be helpful in any way, and listed her many other coping strategies, including writing poetry.

There are kids who find the process of therapy dreary. They find our interest in making things better, talking about problems, and having endless meetings tiresome at best. Call it resistance, denial, or projection. ("It isn't my problem, it's my parents' problem.") As hard as it may be for most of us professionals to believe, therapy is not for everyone. Sometimes the boredom is genuine. Kids like Betsy don't talk in therapy because they aren't ready or willing to make this particular kind of effort. Some may do better talking to friends, writing poetry, playing basketball, working in an animal shelter, dangling from a ledge by a rope, or acting in an improv group. What we call "therapeutic"—sitting and talking in a room—is probably of use and interest to fewer kids than we'd like to believe.

Of course, many kids act bored but aren't. For example, kids with troubled attachment histories frequently try to stay disengaged when they passionately want a relationship. And some teenagers have perfected their air of ennui as a defense against strong feelings. It may take awhile for us to tell the truly bored kids from the very interested but terrified ones. Still, we need to be alert to boredom in any guise; we don't want therapy to be so aversive that a child or adolescent will refuse to return at a later date when she really needs it.

Diagnosis

With Betsy's genetics and disposition, it is quite possible that she *is* headed down the depression road. At this point in her no-talk life, she doesn't demonstrate sufficient dysfunction or motivation to make treatment necessary. Her symptoms can best be explained by an adjustment disorder; she may or may not need treatment later on.

Children sent to therapy by their parents often have dramatically different descriptions of what is happening in their lives from those of their parents. In many cases, they *may* be better prepared to manage snags along the developmental path than their parents believe. This is particularly true for young adolescents, who tend to feel things very deeply but transiently. It is quite common, for example, for a 12-year-old girl to come home on the verge of hysteria about a social problem, creating tremendous anxiety in the household. By the next day, the concerned parents will still be in a lather, but the girl will be on to something else.

At the no-talk end of the continuum, the same child may appear to be in retreat, appearing unusually upset but saying little about it. This can lead to parental fretting and "awfulizing" scenarios; in the absence of real information parents suspect the worst. It may also be true that a more serious problem is brewing. No-talk kids who truly find therapy boring may, like Betsy, have some transient adjustment difficulties, or be somewhat dysthymic. They may also have other problems that might be addressed more readily through other kinds of interventions. These diagnoses include:

- Learning disabilities
- Attention deficit hyperactivity disorder
- Dysthymic disorder
- Parent-child problem
- Adjustment disorder
- No diagnosis

Opposition for Its Own Sake

Diane is a 15-year-old with the air of a seasoned veteran in dealing with adults; she seems to get most of her life's pleasure out of "sassing" them. Her father says that consequences mean nothing to her and that she pushes the envelope of acceptable behavior wherever she goes. Her mother had abandoned the family years earlier and Diane doesn't know where she is. Seemingly willing to come to therapy, once in her seat she stares with pleased defiance. Questions generate smirks and glib answers, and she volunteers nothing. Though she's not an especially bright kid, she's figured out enough about adults' expectations to meet almost none of them. In short, Diane is a pain. She's not really being aggressive but she seems determined to have her fun yanking adult chains and not addressing what brings her into treatment at this time. She's probably angry, under it all, at least as angry as she can make her therapist.

For no-talk kids like Diane, the interest of therapy is in the challenge. Their opposing views keep them engaged with adults in a perverse sort of way. However frustrating and annoying, this connection is real, though it isn't particularly therapeutic. It is virtually impossible to get into problem-solving talk with kids who maintain this stance until they are willing to communicate in some other way.

Diagnosis

Diane easily fit the diagnosis of ODD. I was the recipient of her hostile and negativistic behavior from the outset. But the oppositional-defiant diagnosis didn't explain sufficiently how much Diane was floundering. It only described what she was doing to stay in trouble. Her acting-out concealed a deep sorrow that it took me a while to recognize. Thus she also carried a diagnosis of depression; I explained her limit-testing behavior as a reaction to the grief she felt over losing her mother.

Many kids sent to therapy are, in some way, obnoxious to adults. Some of them have no natural allies. Their disrespectful and unforgiving behaviors prevent even their parents from liking them. The corrective and annoyed reactions they elicit from adults may keep them functioning at the level of a petulant three-year-old who doesn't want to share a toy. No-talk kids who engage only through unpleasantness may, like Diane, have ODD. They may also meet the criteria for one or more of these diagnoses:

- Learning disabilities
- Depression
- Attention deficit hyperactivity disorder
- Oppositional defiant disorder
- Conduct disorder
- Disruptive behavior disorder
- Tourette's disorder
- Post-traumatic stress disorder

Opposition for Power

Seth is 17, and on the surface he's a happy sort of guy. He likes to hang out downtown with his friends and has a girlfriend. While his grades aren't great, he says they are good enough for him. His parents have a completely different story. They report he has not been able to keep several part-time jobs because of a poor work ethic. His friends are all younger and into pot smoking and skateboarding. He is lazy and may fail the year in school. He has been arrested for shoplifting. His girlfriend is just 14 and immature. He doesn't do chores or treat family members respectfully. They are in constant conflict.

To Seth, therapy is just another way his parents are trying to control him. He is affable, but he doesn't really talk in therapy; he sits and smiles and answers questions vaguely, without conviction. He is suspicious of the whole idea of counseling, because he is already feeling overwhelmed and overpowered in other places—no matter what he does, he is criticized. Seth strives for control in the room in the only way available to him at this point. His Alfred E. Neuman "What, me worry?" stance has a certain ferocity to it. Seth is not having fun with his opposition; it's all he can do to hang on.

Many kids do not talk in therapy, because, like Seth, they feel they've been dealt a weak hand in a high-stakes poker game. Sent to therapy against their will by parents, schools, and courts, they feel they have no choice but to play the highest card they have left. It makes no sense to argue or to stand up for themselves, because adults have demonstrated repeatedly that children do not have the last say. Many oppositional kids are more overtly enraged outside of therapy than Seth, and their stony silence is fraught with rage. But whether or not they are acting out elsewhere, they are worthy opponents in therapy. The problem for therapists is that we want to be on the *same* team and need them to disclose something—*anything*—in order to form this precious alliance. Kids who don't talk in therapy because their last shred of self-esteem is on the line will first need to gather some other resources for taking charge of their own lives.

Diagnosis

Seth has three diagnoses: conduct disorder, a substance-related disorder, and dysthymia. He engages in daily antisocial behavior and is also self-medicating for depression. His substance abuse is more frequent and serious than his parents report. All of these diagnoses indicate that he has limited methods for getting through the day. His strategies dig him more deeply into the rut he is trying to escape.

Kids like Seth who perceive reality so differently from their parents are usually in a considerable amount of distress. They haven't developed many methods for managing their lives and seem stuck along the social-emotional runway. Antisocial behavior and drug abuse may leave them functioning further behind their age peers. These no-talk kids may meet the criteria for a range of diagnoses, including, for example:

- Learning disabilities
- Attention deficit hyperactivity disorder
- Oppositional defiant disorder
- Conduct disorder
- Disruptive behavior disorder
- Tourette's disorder
- Major depression
- Substance-related disorders

- Post-traumatic stress disorder
- Reactive attachment disoder

Feeling Trapped

Paula is a 10-year-old girl who has survived a horrendous custody battle between her parents, and sexual abuse by a neighbor
when she was eight. Her father "won" her, and her little sister is
now living four hours away with their mother. Paula has recently
moved in with her father, who is frequently unemployed, and
her chronically ill paternal grandmother, who doesn't really want
either of them in her home, where they cause her stress and
mess up her apartment. Paula has many troubling and regressive
behaviors: she wets the bed, she whines and has tantrums, she
sucks her thumb and twirls her hair, she lies, cheats, and steals.

Paula initially came to family therapy with her father and
grandmother as an eager participant but in just a few weeks began retreating into herself. Therapy became an extension of her
conflicted, emotionally abusive home life, another step in an
endless procession of ever harsher strategies to get her to
change. At their worst, the family meetings were an opportunity
for adults to talk vindictively about how hopeless Paula was. In
one family session, while her grandmother and father were be-
rating her, she pulled her parka over her head and fell sound
asleep.

Kids like Paula discover over time that they have no other
options and withdraw, like turtles under attack. Even a therapy
process that validates both sides of a disagreement serves to
back these kids further into the no-talk corner. Indeed, the neutral position of traditional therapy does little to pull kids from
their shells, because, to them, situations outside the therapy
room are usually much worse than we imagine. Over the course
of the week, they have increasingly fewer options. By the time
they return for a session they are turned even more into no-talk
kids. Paula, and others like her, are silent for survival—a much
more basic need than power.

Diagnosis

Paula's was a traumatized child and I diagnosed her with PTSD. She had frequent nightmares and usually slept on the sofa in the living room. Highly reactive, she would "flip out" under even minor stress. She played alone in a dissociated fantasyland for long periods of time. She couldn't concentrate in school. As long as her home environment was so harsh, it was difficult for her to develop more adaptive strategies for managing her near-constant state of physiological arousal.

The majority of no-talk kids have, in their pasts, trauma of some kind. For these children and adolescents, the consequences of talking and of not talking can be equally perilous. Thus, when kids are trapped traumatically into the no-talk corner we must draw them out of it in a way that ensures their safety at all times. No-talk kids who are this fearful may meet the criteria for the following primary diagnoses:

- Reactive attachment disorder
- Post-traumatic stress disorder
- Anxiety disorder
- Major depression
- Dissociative identity disorder

Shyness

Amanda is an 11-year old girl who blushes when spoken to. She trembles if she has the spotlight in any activity and spends her happiest time with her dogs and cats. Like most shy people, Amanda was probably born that way. She is nearly speechless in therapy, because her physiological response to the intense one-on-one attention is akin to full-blown panic. Her parents want her to become more confident and outgoing, but talk therapy could become just one more demand situation that feels miserable to her.

It is hard for some kids, temperamentally, to be in therapy, even if they want to. A significant body of research (e.g., Kagan,

1984) indicates that about ten percent of kids display this extremely inhibited reaction to novel situations. For them, going
to therapy can feel like punishment, putting their perceived inadequacy on display. Extreme shyness does have consequences
for how kids are treated by their teachers and peers and how
they will get their needs met. However, therapy aimed at *elim-
inating* this trait has as much chance of succeeding as treatment
for eye color. Shy kids can learn to calm themselves and even to
assert themselves a bit more, but they will not alter their basic
way of being in the world.

An extreme form of shyness is evident in children who are
(s)elective mutes. These kids may speak normally at home, with
family members, but be completely silent at school and in the
community. Elective mutes are the most ferocious no-talk kids
around. The more adults try to cajole, bribe, or trick them into
talking, the more intractable the problem becomes. It's possible
that they're so shy that they can't bear for others to hear the
sound of their voices. Demands for speech cause them to become physiologically overaroused, and they cope by shutting
down completely. Trauma can also turn some kids into elective
mutes—they become shy and anxious when attention is focused
on them. By definition, treatment of these children has to be no-
talk therapy. But we can only help shy kids of any stripe when
we take into consideration how arduous it is for them to be
successful in a talking world.

Diagnosis
Amanda's fearful style of interacting with the world clearly indicated that she was an anxious child. I diagnosed her with a nonspecific anxiety disorder.

Even class clowns and actors can be shy and anxious people.
Johnny Carson, for example, describes himself as painfully shy.
Therapists often find themselves treating kids who have been
acting-out at school but are tongue-tied in the office. In these
cases, the acting out serves as a cover for the painful feelings of
shyness. More often, however, shy or mute kids are referred pre-

cisely because of their anxiety about talking out loud. They look and act shy, and the history supports this description. While these kids may well have developed problems associated with shyness, it is important not to pathologize a physiologically-based, and essentially "normal," way of being in the world. However, they may also meet criteria for several diagnoses, including:

- Learning disabilities
- Reactive attachment disorder
- Post-traumatic stress disorder
- Separation anxiety disorder
- Selective mutism
- Pervasive developmental disorder
- Obsessive compulsive disorder
- Other anxiety disorder
- Sensory integration problems

Disengagement

Martin is a severely depressed and angry 14-year-old boy who wants to be left alone. He has been sent by his parents and school, against his will, to therapy, and though he doesn't say much, he doesn't conceal his dissatisfaction—he glowers and sneers. He's in trouble for truancy, petty theft, and smoking pot before school. Martin is not just silent—he's antisocial. He picks apart his sneaker and threads from his jeans, bites his nails, and shreds his Styrofoam cup—all onto the floor. He's pushing people away whether he knows it or not; his unwillingness to talk creates a moat around him. He stares vacantly, answers questions in a mumble, and leaves without saying goodbye. He's already gotten rid of several therapists with this highly effective strategy. His divorced parents refuse to be together in the same room. In parent-child sessions with each of them, they give basically the same concerned lectures while he sits there passively. Martin wants to be left alone with his depression. People tell him what to do *and* how to do it, and he has little personal investment in his own life.

Alienated teenagers like Martin don't have the sense that what they have to contribute has an impact or matters; adults have all the say, anyway. These kids feel disconnected from their own lives and, as an extension, the process of therapy. Many disengaged adolescents live with this intense inability to put their angst into words. Traditional therapy cannot tap into the depths of their despair. Parents and therapists alike succumb to the temptation to tell them, "I understand how you feel." We attempt, in vain, to match our own youthful experiences to theirs, unaware that this pairing actually diminishes them, pushing them further into silent alienation. Their specialness, it seems, lies in their estrangement—and this ability to withstand the onslaught of connecting language may be their most cherished defense.

Diagnosis

Martin's drug use was concerning, and he had emerging features of a conduct disorder, if not an antisocial personality disorder. But his depression also stood out as a dominant issue for treatment. This boy was drowning in inadequate strategies for managing his feelings of pain and hopelessness. He had so little success in his life that surviving each day was an accomplishment all its own.

When no-talk kids reach such a level of disconnection that it becomes a way of life, it is likely that they have surpassed the James Dean rebel phase and are at severe risk for a future on the margins. These kids may appear, despite their youth, to have a deeply antisocial way about them, and their anguish can be buried under substance use, delinquent acting-out, icy disregard for others, and a prevailing sense that the world is a violent, irrational place. They may carry heavy Axis II personality disorders on top of the relatively more benign and treatable problems of other no-talkers. And while their offending behavior may get them the most attention, they are also frequently traumatized.

From a developmental perspective, these kids may function as egocentric infants, able to focus only on getting their immediate needs met. Their attachments, if they have any, are primitive,

self-serving and transient. As adolescents, they may be quite
promiscuous, with little interest in self-protection. Disengaged
kids like Martin may meet the criteria for a veritable textbook of
diagnoses, depending upon the function and intensity of their
acting-out behaviors:

- Learning disabilities
- Attention deficit hyperactivity disorder
- Oppositional defiant disorder
- Conduct disorder
- Disruptive behavior disorder
- Tourette's disorder
- Major depression
- Substance-related disorders
- Post-traumatic stress disorder
- Reactive attachment disorder
- Personality disorder (e.g., paranoid, schizoid, antisocial, borderline)

It should be evident from these case vignettes that no-talk
kids come in every size, shape, and hue of the rainbow. They are
depressed and enraged, anxious and confused, delinquent and
terrified. Many have learning and attention problems. The com-
plexity of life that leads them to a therapist's office requires mul-
tidimensional assessment and a variety of perspectives. A thorough evaluation is critical for good diagnosis *and* effective
treatment planning.

EVALUATING THE NO-TALK KID

Observations

With kids who won't tell us what's wrong, we're apt to become
like the blind men with the elephant, each describing only what
is right in front of him. For this reason, we need to take our
observations on the road, to assess what is happening in a vari-

ety of settings and situations. We want to know about the problems, of course, and their exceptions, and different stories about
how the child or adolescent has come to have such a hard time.
But, beyond the more obvious intake-interview-type questions,
we also want to get a sense of the whole person. A major goal of
observation, then, is to find some basis for empathic connection—in pleasure as well as in pain. We need to be able to say,
"If I were this child, I would do exactly as he does." Possible
observations might include:

Family
- The child alone: Usually, since we don't know any better,
  we proceed with rapport-building strategies, gathering information as though this were a talking kid. What happens
  when our "standard techniques" fall flat? How does this
  child manage the initial sessions differently from what we
  expected? What does the silence seem to indicate right off?
- The child with parents: What is the quality and quantity of
  interaction between the child and the parent(s)? How do
  they get him to speak? Are they successful? What kinds of
  conversation engage him or shut him down?
- Parent(s) alone: How far apart are the child and parents on
  how they view the problem? How empathic are the parents
  to the child's experience of what is happening? How does
  the background information support or complicate current
  observations? How do the parents' own difficulties affect
  their child? The distance between perspectives can contribute to the child's unwillingness to speak. He may feel there
  is no common language anymore.
- The child with siblings: How did this particular child in the
  family come to have the identified problem? Is there a potentially helpful or destructive sibling relationship? Is there
  conversation between the child and the sibling(s)? If so,
  what do they talk about? How does the sibling view the
  child? The problem?

- The whole family together: What happens to the child when all are assembled together? Does the child participate more or less when the family is present? How are communication patterns, secrets, and silences in the family mirrored and magnified by the no-talk kid?
- Extended family (e.g., aunts, uncles, cousins, grandparents): Are there others in the family who can shed more light on the situation and lend support to the child? What is the quality and nature of their relationship?
- Home visits: If the explanation for the problem remains hazy, a home visit can often clear up the question. What is it like to live in that home, with those people? How does this environment shape the no-talk attitude? Does the child or adolescent converse more freely at home?

Peers
- Social observations in school: How does the child manage herself socially during the day? In classes, at recess, at lunch, at the bus stop? Do other kids approach her? What happens when she interacts with peers throughout the day? Is this an area of relative strength or weakness for her? How does the child appear compared with the local culture of the school and peers? Does she fit in? Is there a match between her and a group of other kids?
- Inviting friends to the office: Sometimes no-talk kids are willing to bring in friends who can do some of the talking for them. Some are more willing to talk when a friend is there for support. This is particularly true for adolescents. What kind of support do these friends offer? Are the friends struggling in their own lives? Does the child have anyone to invite?
- After-school activities: Does the child participate in any extracurricular activities in school or the community? What is the nature and extent of this involvement? Are there any potential community connections that are immediately obvious?

School

- Different classes: How does the child manage different subjects and teachers? Where does he sit in the room, and how is this affecting his ability to succeed there?
- Structured and unstructured times: How does the child handle the different degrees of structure and support offered through the day? Are there some times and places in school that seem particularly difficult? Easy? What is his level of organization? Does he seem to have learning or attention problems in school?
- Transitions: What happens during in-between times? Does the child appear to get lost, have exceptional problems, or become stressed during transitions? How much help does he require to get from place to place, subject to subject? How does he handle room to move and use the physical spaces at school?
- With teachers: How do teachers approach the child? How many times is the child's name used in a half-hour? (Go back in a couple of months and do this observation again to see how your intervention has changed that.)
- Bulletin boards: How does displayed work compare with the child's art and writing? How does the child fit with the local norms?

Neighborhood

- Knowing the context: What is the neighborhood like? Who, if anyone, lives nearby? How long has the family lived there? How much does the child feel she is part of the home and neighborhood? What degree of safety, satisfaction, and connection to community is there?
- Natural supports already in place: Outside the family, who is there for the no-talk kid? Are there friends and neighbors available to help?
- Potential local resources: Does the neighborhood have some services available for kids of this age? What are they

(Scouts, jobs, Y programs, a rec center, after-school and summer programs, Project Adventure, church youth groups, etc.)?

Observing children while collecting information from so many sources gives us the chance to get to know them on their own terms and in their own places. Observation provides us with valuable information to aid in both diagnosis and treatment. While we're seeing the no-talk kid in different contexts, we're considering how to make therapy successful and getting to know what resources are available for him in his family, school, and community. Naturally, we aren't the only ones doing the observing; it's likely that we're be scrutinized just as thoroughly by the no-talk kid.

Playing

The assessment period with a no-talk kid should be fun. If it is too serious, the transition to the therapy proper will be awkward, if not doomed altogether. Given the premise that no-talk kids have developmental delays in one or more areas, we can also imagine that only the most disengaged or terrified adolescent will turn down a chance to play a little. Indeed, a no-talk *and* no-play kid (who isn't comatose) is likely cause for particular concern. Thus, from the moment the dialogue grinds to a halt, the evaluation will need to include some basic fun stuff, including the best of a traditional play therapy set-up. The Appendix is full of activities to engage no-talk kids.

Projective Questions
These include more fun and nondirective kinds of queries: What are your three wishes? If you had a magic wand, what would you change about your life? What animal would you want to be? (Or, for teenagers: If there is reincarnation, what person or animal would you want to come back as?) What is the best age to

be? Who would you want to be stuck on a desert island with? What is your favorite joke? If you had a million dollars, what would you do?

Activities

If kids won't talk, they may be willing to do some diverting things with you: shared storytelling (taking turns with the plotline); drawings of people, places, favorite things and occasions; building a model together; or engaging in some other cooperative project. Any of these simple activities constitutes communication, albeit via the back door.

Games

Children of an astonishing range of ages are willing to play games with an adult, including therapeutic and traditional board games, card games, Nerf ball games, and computer games. The point is not whether the activity is, in some very specific sense, therapeutic, but whether it provides more information about how the child copes in the world and relates to others than can be collected in strained silence. Game-playing also honors a child's agenda, engaging her on familiar terms.

Play Assessment

The no-talk therapist's office looks a lot like any other play therapy room, with the addition of games and activities that teenagers might also be willing to engage in, as well as assorted materials for projects. The available supplies may include: puppets, large dolls, a dollhouse with several human and animal families, baby bottle and blanket, pretend food and dishes, construction and drawing paper, paints, markers, crayons and colored pencils (including a fancy set with nice drawing paper for teenagers), tape, glue, scissors, and staples, clay or Play Doh, blocks, Legos, Lincoln Logs, Tinkertoys or other construction supplies, sandbox or sand tray, wild and domestic plastic animal families, play phones, cash register with play money, stuffed animals, Matchbox cars, doctor's bag, puzzles, and kits/supplies for projects (e.g., model cars, jewelry, stationery, Popsicle-stick boxes, magic shows).

In the play assessment, as in play therapy, the materials are invitingly available, and the child or adolescent takes the lead, with the therapist following and joining. Play can be a most revealing window into functioning; it's also fun and beats sitting around feeling anxious.

Assessment and the Circle of Adults

From the moment of referral, a therapist becomes part of the circle of adults in a child's life. For no-talk kids, this needs to become a stated and intentional support structure. Ideally, part of the assessment process will include a meeting with the child and the involved adults to begin identifying concerns and roles. Because we only see kids once or twice a week (or even less frequently) for an hour, we need to remember that our participation on a team will strengthen everything we do. Members of the starting circle might include:

- Family members
- Friends and neighbors
- Teachers and school personnel
- Pediatricians/other medical specialists
- Probation officers/guardian ad litem/lawyers
- Child protection workers
- Past therapists
- Big Brothers/Big Sisters
- Clergy
- Respite care workers
- Anyone else whom the parents (and the child) identify as potential sources of support.

Other Assessment Methods

Even after we complete a variety of observations, convene the circle of adults, and play a bit, some no-talk kids remain enigmatic. Occasionally, the explanations that we can develop through these methods aren't sufficient for us to get treatment into high gear. Luckily, more information can be collected. It is fascinating to note that many kids who are unwilling to talk will happily fill out the hundreds of items on the adolescent version of the Minnesota Multiphasic Personality Inventory or the similarly lengthy Personality Inventory for Youth.

School Reports

A child's school record, including the results of standardized testing, is often a font of valuable information. Over the years, the school file accumulates a picture of learning and attention problems, intellectual potential, developmental concerns, and deteriorating performance, all of which are quite informative in the case of no-talk kids. The school record may also have notes sent home, nurse's reports, a record of latenesses and absences, notes sent in by parents, and other informal documentation of a child's school life—all descriptive of how the child is functioning in this most important realm.

Previous Treatment Records

It is always helpful to speak with past therapists and obtain notes and reports from them. Because no-talk kids may go through a number of different therapists over time, this documentation is very useful. Learning what went wrong in previous therapy enables us to make our own mistakes.

Medical and Hospital Records

No-talk kids may have concomitant medical problems, and significant medical histories. The most common medical bases for emotional problems include: vision and hearing difficulties, learning disabilities, attention deficit disorder, sleep problems, substance abuse, depression, undiagnosed allergies, lack of exercise, and undetected child abuse (Hallowell, 1996). Medical records also include interesting information about who brings kids for visits and how often, whether they are really ill or not at appointments, whether immunizations are up to date, and the physician's concerns about the child. A collaborative relationship with the family doctor or pediatrician is often vital to no-talk therapy—especially for kids who have problems that also require medical attention.

Psychological Assessment
Formal psychological evaluation can be extremely useful with no-talk kids. For psychologists who have access to these measurement tools, the relationship that develops over the course of the testing can actually facilitate therapy. For nonpsychologists, the evaluator can share information useful in treatment planning and become another person in the circle of adults. In general, psychological assessment covers the following areas:

- *Behavior rating scales* (e.g., Achenbach Child Behavior Checklist, Connors Scales, Vineland Adaptive Behavior Scale) provide more objective data about a child than observation and interviewing can offer.
- *Personality assessment* (e.g., Personality Inventory for Youth, Piers-Harris Children's Self-Concept Scale, Millon Adolescent Personality Inventory, Minnesota Multiphasic Personality Inventory-Adolescent form) gives us more of a handle on the emotional functioning and interpersonal style of children and adolescents.
- *Projective testing* (e.g., Rorschach, Thematic Apperception Test, House-Tree-Person Drawings, Kinetic Family Drawing) offers a subjective window into the unconscious per-

ceptions and defensive style that a no-talk kid may bring to therapy.

- *Emotional testing* (e.g., Manifest Anxiety Scales, Children's Depression Inventory) provides empirical and specific self-report information about how a child is feeling.
- *Achievement testing* (e.g., Wide Range Achievement Test, Woodcock-Johnson Tests of Achievement, Wechsler Individual Achievement Test) gives some insight into a child's learning style and academic strengths and weaknesses.
- *Intelligence testing* (e.g., Wechsler Intelligence Scales for Children-3rd Edition, Woodcock-Johnson Tests of Cognitive Ability, Kaufman Assessment Battery for Children) provides important information about cognitive strengths and weaknesses, including possible evidence of difficulty with the verbal reasoning required by traditional therapy.
- *Neuropsychological assessment* (e.g., Halstead Reitan, Luria's Neuropsychological Investigation) establishes a relationship between brain functioning and behavior and offers more precise information about intellectual strengths and weaknesses.

When all parts of the assessment are completed, we should have a coherent explanation for why the child or adolescent is not talking in therapy and some promising strategies for intervention. It's then time to let the wild rumpus begin.

8

No-Problem Therapy

UNLIKE TRADITIONAL treatment, in no-talk therapy we make little practical distinction between the period of assessment and formal therapy. We may have a set plan for data collection, but we'll also need some back-up ideas about what else we might do. Although we want to evaluate the child and situation, in the initial weeks we are also laying the foundation for how we'll be working. In practice, then, the diagnostic strategies and the interventions may well be the same. But the individual child or adolescent *must* be more important to us than the Diagnostic and Statistical Manual. The *explanation*, not the diagnosis, guides the intervention. We often have to dive straight into a no-talk activity. Thus, when kids aren't talking, treatment can even *precede* diagnosis.

No-talk kids give us plenty of feedback about whether we're on the right track with them. This is reassuring, albeit in a perverse sort of way; when one approach fizzles, we *can* change plans and try again. We begin only with the four "H's": a little History, a few Hunches, some Hope, and a few Helpful ideas about how to make some initial connections. And then we watch how the kids react.

Lack of specific preparation doesn't always mean a long first hour. Sometimes referring agents or parents warn us, in no uncertain terms, that a particular child will not speak in the therapy. We prepare ourselves for the great wait. But when she arrives, the dam bursts in moments, and we're faced with just the opposite dilemma—it's hard to *end* the session. At other times, though, armed with some usual introductory protocol, we realize we're doing *all* the talking and hence, all the work. Many other kids fall somewhere in between; they seem to want to engage— they're present in the room—even if they're not particularly adept at making connections. For most, we still have to find the right fly in our tackle box, but at least we know there's a fish to catch. Although an occasional kid won't bite, no matter what alluring specimen we throw out, these are relatively rare cases.

FROM ASSESSMENT TO TREATMENT

No-talk kids tend to have no idea why we want to ask them about their misery. They may be convinced we're out to to get them with our diagnostic interviews and history-of-the-problem questions. Often (and rightfully so), they're expecting the worst—more depressing, despicable inquiries about their bad deeds and restrictive "behavior contracts" to squeeze them into doing better.

If we treat them alone, we run the risk of putting kids in the "hot seat" with so much attention that they're uncomfortable, or even terrified. But if we include parents in an opening session, we're likely to hear a lot of negative and embarrassing information that taints our connection from the outset. After all, most people want to make a good first impression, and no-talk kids don't usually have much chance of that. So each decision we make brings its hazards.

Sometimes we want to please concerned parents who perceive

therapy as a place to get things out in the open, right away. Adults are used to going to doctors and leaving with a prescription or a cast or a set plan for how a body will get better. To most, therapy should be just like that, which puts us in a quandary as we try to establish a relationship with a no-talk kid. If we attend to the parents' pressing needs to talk about their concerns, we paint a no-talk kid deep into the corner. When we tell parents we don't want to hear about a lot of negative stuff, they're often skeptical; how can we fix something we don't know is broken? Often, like a musician practicing, we need to have several "first sessions" before we get it right; if we're allowed the luxury of time, we can often work our way through the tough introductory rhythms.

It's a leap, even for child therapists, to get past the notion that we have to talk about problems to solve them. It's still harder for parents to accept their kids' legitimate limitations doing therapy. They often say, "I hope you can get him to open up. He won't tell me what is wrong." The dilemma for the first session goes beyond educating parents about child development—though this is often a good place to begin. It really extends to the question of who sets the agenda for what will happen in the room. The parents have rights—they pay the bills, they're worried about their kids. The no-talk kids have rights—they're the ones being asked to change and to do work they can't or won't do. The therapists have rights—and an obligation—to have a theory about why a given opening gambit makes sense to try with this kid at this time. We're expected to have a method to our madness, even when we're winging it. Of course, we set some of the agenda by drawing on our professional expertise. For example, we may refuse to have family sessions if parents insist on using the time to list all the horrors of the past week. But, somehow, we also have to work to hear everyone's voices, whether or not they are audible.

Thus, a variety of opening moves may work for a given no-talk kid and her family, sometimes in combinations unique to the child and circumstances. But it is important to view sessions that fall flat as opportunities for curiosity and learning. Happily, kids can be remarkably forgiving.

Lack of Skill

When kids, like Colin, described in chapter 7 (see p. 108), are developmentally delayed and traumatized, data collection needs to proceed from several angles. On the phone, before the first meeting, I tried to ascertain what Colin enjoyed playing with, and I arranged to have that available. I received a huge stack of school, medical, and placement records, and began to assemble as detailed a timeline as possible. Even if kids can't remember much in the past, we need to hold onto this history as the backdrop to events that may unfold during their time with us. Colin's information-processing problems jumped from these pages; I arranged for a formal psychological evaluation at the school after we met for the first time. I also visited Colin at school as part of the early assessment and treatment; I saw first-hand how distractible and labor-intensive he was for his teacher, his significant social immaturity, and his determination. I met with his foster parents, pediatrician, teacher, social worker, and school counselor and we became his "team," exchanging information frequently over the course of treatment. All this early work both created and developed my role in the support structure around this vulnerable little boy.

The first session was simple and informal. I kept a couple of toys out and the rest tucked away—I wanted the room to look inviting but not too overwhelming. I spent the hour with him on the floor, even though his foster parents wanted to sit in chairs. I knew that Colin loved to play with Matchbox cars. He entered the room and barely acknowledged me before excitedly dumping out the bucket of cars that sat temptingly on the rug. Although he was unaccustomed to playing with someone else, my spot on the floor became a predictable part of the routine we established. Sitting next to Colin, I was able to speak to his preadoptive parents while also beginning, indirectly, to make myself available to him. I'd hand him cars or ask him which was his favorite. I also set out my rescue vehicles, letting him know that we could handle crashes in this office.

One of the most important aspects of the first session is giving kids some hope to take away with them. If they leave unchanged and untouched, they may not be willing to return, or they may sink deeper into the no-talk quagmire. It is important to find one place where we can make a difference right off. Colin, not surprisingly, had a large number of fears that caused him to panic and interfered with his ability to go to sleep at night. His foster mother noted that he worried most about fire and not being able to escape if the house began to burn down. In the first session, I gave him one strategy for handling his fear of fire.

It was senseless to interpret Colin's fears in light of his trauma history or even to introduce him to cognitive-behavioral strategies that might soothe his thoughts. The intervention had to make sense for a pudgy little blond kid making loud car noises on the floor, exhibiting no curiosity about the adults in the room, with the functional vocabulary of a three-year-old. The options were limited. Combing through his routines like a detective, I discovered that Colin liked to sing in the bathtub. Better yet, he usually had a broad smile on his face when he sang. I had the opening I needed. Colin agreed to try to sing when he was worrying about fire to see if that would help him feel better. His foster mother said she would get him started and join him for the finale of "I've Been Workin' on the Railroad." They left singing together.

With unskilled kids, consistency and predictability are essential. Too much change or variability can produce anxiety and mistrust. So I arranged my room similarly the next time Colin came. He went to his spot, and I plunked down in mine. We met without his mother and began to establish a way of being together that felt increasingly comfortable and warm. For many, many weeks we sat near each other on the floor, making car noises, lining cars up in different groupings, and comparing cars.

This activity was a mental stretch for me; even the first hour had its tedious repetitions. But while tuning into his passion for cars I began to notice subtle changes in his play. He'd push a car out into the center and wait for me to copy him. He'd hold a car up and expect me to make a comment about it. He'd take all the "good guy" cars, and I'd find myself with all the "bad guys." He'd start where we left off the preceding week. As I fostered Colin's interest with curiosity and persistence of my own, he became more responsive to me, too.

Over many weeks we sang, made snacks, played with cars and Legos, and occasionally tried to play with puppets. For a child with so much instability in his life, I offered him sameness month after month. The gains were entirely modest but, over a couple of *years*, steady. Fears abated, massive tantrums came and went, and he endured three separate school placements. Colin retained precious few events in his life, claiming no memory even for things that had happened hours earlier. But he began to develop self-soothing strategies, like singing, counting, and breathing deeply, learned a little about the give-and-take of friendship and acquired some basic trust. For a boy with so many problems and so few skills, each of these minor achievements was a kind of triumph.

In general, no-talk therapy with kids who lack the skills necessary for symbolic play or language will proceed without much fanfare and hoopla. There is no substitute for time, especially when developmental delays are compounded by a troubled attachment history. We do things with the kids and behind the scenes to help them cope more effectively, but our steady presence in their lives is often the most therapeutic intervention we offer.

Boredom

Many kids sent to therapy are prepared to be more bored than they'd be at the opera. The whole notion of spending an hour talking with some well-dressed grown-up about deeply personal feelings is not one of the top 100 things they want to do. But, on first evaluation, it's not generally clear if a particular bored kid is someone who: (1) needs therapy, so we should work to engage; (2) needs some kind of extra support, but not therapy, so we should refer to a rock-climbing school, a theater program, a volunteer program at a day-care center, or some other place that will function as a therapeutic environment in a less obvious way; (3) needs therapy, but not right now; or (4) is really doing fine and is bored because, well, we're boring.

Clearly, we don't have to treat everyone who comes through our door. We need to decide if we have something to offer the mildly depressed 12-year-old who yawns through the hour, the jaded adolescent who arrives late and leaves early, the nine-year-old who wants to do her homework during the session so she can watch *Rescue Rangers* when she gets home; or the hyper seven-year-old who starts painting his hands green when his picture is done. In some circumstances, each of these kids can come around to being an ideal no-talk-therapy kid. Boredom can be an invitation to us to change the framework so that it is different from their expectations—i.e., more fun than opera. But there are times when options 2, 3, or 4 are more realistic and likely to be helpful—times when therapy just isn't the best solution.

Betsy, the bored 12-year-old with a family history of depression (see p. 110) would have kept coming to treatment if her parents had insisted upon it. She might even have found it comforting at times, but the risks were considerable. She might turn against therapy and be unwilling to consider it if she really needed to speak to someone at a later date. She might also begin to view her biological loading as destiny and become less self-reliant and confident at a vulnerable stage in her early adolescence. Perhaps worst of all, she could continue to find therapy boring and irrelevant.

We need to establish early on whether therapy will be the most effective intervention for bored kids. We can usually discover this in a couple of sessions. If we're still unclear about the need after we take a detailed history from the concerned parents and see the child, we can do a school visit or get some testing done. With Betsy, the first hour with her parents was quite useful because I got to observe her reactions to their concerns. Although she was not particularly responsive or forthcoming, I did get the sense that she was listening to them and that her retreat wasn't extreme. While she spent more time in her room than she had at younger ages, she was involved at school with friends, writing for the school magazine, and playing softball. I didn't have the sense that she was seriously depressed, though she did have a dramatic flair.

In the following session, with Betsy alone, she reassured me further that she wasn't suicidal and had a variety of mechanisms for coping with her sad feelings. We established some guidelines about which concerns would lead her back to therapy—greater depression, increased trouble with friends, substance use—and agreed that her parents could continue to get support for their worries, if they desired.

In fact, her parents decided that *they* would attend sessions from time to time, to discuss adolescent development and keep tabs on their sense of how Betsy was managing. We all concurred that she could enter therapy at some other time when it might seem more useful, if not more intriguing. With bored kids like Betsy, the door stays open because we can't predict if developmental changes will make therapy more appealing at a later date. From a family systems perspective, continuing work with her parents could result in lasting benefits to Betsy. And since no-talk therapy is pragmatic, we're willing to work with parents and other concerned adults, as well as with kids who won't talk.

Overall, children and adolescents who are prepared for boredom are hard to engage. Occasionally, they're pleasantly surprised that therapy isn't as tedious as they anticipated. But many kids who have mastered the weary eye roll will be determined to fend off any connections they see headed their way, making therapy harder—and less absorbing—for everyone. We'll spend a huge amount of time trying to be charming and useful, and they'll rummage in their pockets, toss a pillow in the air, or twist paperclips into sharp weapons. If we truly believe that therapy will offer them better self-soothing, problem-solving, and relationship skills than they can get elsewhere, then we should persevere. But for many of them, we'd better pull out the Rolodex and start making referrals to interesting programs or simply suggest that we should be in touch in a couple of months to discuss how it's going.

Opposition for Its Own Sake

Kids who are witnesses to violence, divorce, and betrayal, participants in shifting, unpredictable relationships, or just uncertain about how to engage honestly with someone else seem to enter relationships as though playing a chess game, trying to anticipate the next move. They bring to therapy the expectation that people are not to be trusted and have ulterior motives when they are kind; however, at the same time (and like most people), they probably don't want to feel so isolated.

With some no-talk kids, the conflict between feelings of suspicion and a need for contact sets up a tension that is palpable from the outset. These kids tend to be annoying, harsh, and sarcastic, but they're not bored. They may refuse to disclose referral information, saying something like, "You're the doctor, you tell me why I'm here," or "Wake me up when you're finished"— comments designed to get a response, but not a conversation. For these kids, the novelty of the therapy is also very disconcerting. Not knowing the rules or procedures, they get their backs up in a defensive hurry.

Diane, the 15-year-old toughie (see p. 112), engaged in therapy through a series of wise-ass comments, behaviors, and suggestions that simultaneously pulled me in and kept me away. For example, she always arrived early for appointments but would feign fascination with a magazine article so I would have to sit there in the waiting room until *she* was ready. She'd wear headphones and wait, bopping to her private music, until I demanded she remove them. She also had a field day mocking my shoe selection; I tried to feel encouraged that she noticed me at all. Although she was unwilling to have a conversation with me, Diane had perfected the wilting one-liner. I'd say into the silence, "It might be fun to do a project." She'd sneer, "Is that what floats your ice?" Or I'd tell her when our next appointment was, and say I'd see her then. She'd roll her eyes and reply, "Not if I see you first." Diane only seemed to talk when her comments could silence me.

Stymied, I met with Diane's father a couple of times in the early weeks to try and make sense of how to proceed. He had few expectations for his daughter. Unlike her perky and over-achieving younger sister, Diane didn't have many friends and had rarely done well in school. Reviewing her academic history, I noted she had been an uninspired student throughout her career. Her mother, who was reportedly traveling around as a free spirit, went years at a stretch without even sending a postcard—an unspeakable loss for Diane. After her father remarried and divorced a second time, Diane just seemed to harden and bump along on the periphery for many years. She had been dropped to low-level classes that provided little challenge and virtually no homework. The phone didn't ring for her. She didn't participate in any after-school activities and simply watched a string of soap operas every afternoon when she got home; indeed, she attempted to schedule her appointments around the airing of *General Hospital*. (In desperation, I considered watching it with her; no-talk therapy *is* about following the child's interests, and the soaps do have provocative themes. Fortunately, I was spared this fate, though it was good to have *General Hospital* as a back-up option.)

The referral came from a school guidance counselor who was concerned that Diane was falling through the cracks and not taking hold anywhere. She was in jeopardy of failing the year and seemed depressed. With background stories like this one, oppositional kids need extra time and nurturing to become engaged with us. We put in hours with these kids, absorbing their psychic stabs and coming back for more, accepting the evidence that they have great reason to be wary and suspicious. This is not to suggest that we need to endure abuse silently, but rather to note that the verbal sparring is how they connect—it is the text of therapy. Our subtext, all the while, is: I understand, I care, I can find pleasure in being with you, I see through this.

I kept tabs on my frustration, continued to stay empathic for the most part, and hung in with this uncomfortable way of being together. I stuck to my firm belief that she secretly wanted to be with me, but was wildly inept. Occasionally, I'd peel an orange and share it with her, make a bowl of popcorn and pass it over, toss her a wad of clay to squish. Once, by accident, I spilled my tea all over the table and I got her to help me mop it up. She was delighted to partake in my mishap. I tried to keep my confidence up because she wasn't protesting to her father about coming. She still seemed to enjoy making fun of me.

Diane's therapy progressed on three fronts. First, I spent time trying to discover what interested her in the world. Although it didn't "float my ice," she expressed a desire to become a funeral director someday. She knew about the occupation from a second cousin already in this line of work. Together, we arranged for her to volunteer in his funeral home and, when she turned 16, to be paid to assist in the office and with visiting hours. (Diane was willing to do this once she made arrangements to tape the soap operas she would miss.) Through this job, she made friends with another teenager who worked there and began to develop an identity as someone who had skills and a future.

The second area of development was the formation of basic trust and some perspective that enabled her to look at herself with greater humor and warmth. My effusive interest in her also appealed to her adolescent self-absorption. I *knew* she was dressing up to see me, and I commented on every new thing. Also, although she succeeded in getting under my skin from time to time, her commentary on *my* life was usually hilarious, and *I* became more proficient at ducking and bobbing around her occasional barbs and persevering with her. In fact, my shoes *were*, as she described, "like *soooo* two years ago."

In turn, my resilience and the rhythm of therapy offered Diane a safe place to practice both her wit and a softer way of relating. The funeral work with grieving people also opened untold opportunities for her to begin her journey mourning the loss of her all-but-dead mother. She didn't bring any of these connections into my office, but she did note proudly that she was getting a lot of praise for her gentle and empathic work during visiting hours at the funeral home.

After a few months of this oppositional engagement, Diane ventured slowly into the third aspect of the therapy—problem-solving. She indicated that she was ready one day, by offering the first of many glimpses into her life, and how hard it was. "My Spanish teacher is a butthead and I'm not doing the detention," she said and then refused to say more. And, on another day, "It's so unfair that my sister gets to stay out 'til 11 and I never did." A couple of weeks later: "There's a party and I'm not invited but I don't even care." For Diane, getting through a day meant hauling huge sacks of sadness around. It was enough for her, during these early months, to heave them at my feet, without daring to open them up. Any follow-up questions I was foolish enough to ask caused her to shrink back and make a crack about my nosiness, my inadequacy, or my fashion choices.

In the final months of regularly scheduled treatment, she allowed me to go with her to talk to her teachers, role play certain peer problems, have family meetings to discuss rules for both of the girls, and even direct her attention into the "sacks" so we could empty them. From time to time she would acknowledge when she was upset, usually with some reluctance; she never wanted to sort through the particulars. Such depth work could wait until she was an adult; this was her therapy, on her terms. To underscore this point, even when I was seeing her once a month or less frequently, Diane would begin sessions by refusing to change her tactics. She knew that I would sit nearby, patiently, while she finished the compelling article about Leonardo DiCaprio she was reading in the waiting room. It didn't matter to me where we were "doing" this therapy; the waiting room was clearly as good as my office for Diane.

The point of no-talk therapy with kids who engage through oppositional maneuvers is to honor their defensive *and* offensive strategies. Even as we scrap our agendas for "therapy" for a time, we can see how singularly vital the relationship itself is for them and let them attend to it in the ways they know how. We can't make them talk, play, or even come to the room until they are good and ready, so persistence and pacing count for much of the groundwork with them. These are kids who have mastered the preemptive strike. They are convinced that they will be treated poorly, abandoned, and forgotten. Our resolve to keep trying has to be even stronger than their determination to dump us first.

Opposition for Power

Some kids are really just furious, and many have good reason. They may demonstrate their rage through explosive and defiant behaviors, passive withdrawal, or systematic noncompliance, but, whatever their style, the result is the same. They don't want to come to therapy, they don't want to talk to anyone, and they absolutely don't want to hear what anyone has to say to them. The power imbalance they experience with adults is severe. These kids respond to therapy the way they do to all other demand situations at home, at school, and in the community: *forget it*. Attending therapy is most certainly not their idea, and they want us to keep this fact in mind while we think of ways to get them to interact with us or deal more constructively with their lives.

Seth, the 17-year-old slacker (see p. 114), was in many ways as enraged as any no-talk kid, even though he didn't generally act angry in treatment. Of course, he simmered some when his parents attended sessions, but for the most part he grinned his way through any requests made of him. He controlled his life by not caring about it—the more adults threatened, cajoled, and established consequences, the more *laissez-faire* his approach became. Curfew at 12? He waltzed in at 2 a.m. Teachers sending him to detention? Once seated, he read a comic book. Needed to watch his younger brother? He didn't come home at all. He'd agree with any reasonable argument about how he might improve his behavior—and then do *exactly as he pleased*. In family sessions, he defended himself without conviction, complained that his parents were on his back, and left smiling. In early individual meetings, he answered questions without malice or commitment. He knew how to kill an hour painlessly. And he also got little out of being there.

At 17, Seth was beyond the point where adults' threatened consequences had much bite in them. He had to begin taking responsibility for himself, setting his own goals and authoring his own life. The moment that therapy began to resemble real-world powerlessness for him, he became blander than Wonder bread. Paradoxically, he seized control by disappearing even as he sat there. And he held onto power tenaciously, like a terrier with a sock, wagging his tail at one end and clenching down furiously at the other.

Seth also seemed quite developmentally delayed in his lack of compassion for the people who cared about him. He acted coldly and harshly, for example, telling his mother she needed to be institutionalized when she cried with worry about him, and spraining his younger, smaller brother's arm in a fight. Afterwards, he wouldn't apologize, commenting, "He needed to learn a lesson; I did him a favor by hurting him. He'll know better next time." Yet, I had the sense that Seth didn't feel he could win in other, kinder ways. He desperately needed opportunities to extend some good will toward others.

My assessment of Seth's situation took place on four fronts. I interviewed him with his family, spoke to him alone, met with him and his girlfriend, and administered some tests to look at his substance abuse, social problems, and underlying depression. After the family meeting, where the two versions of his competence were delineated (Seth's view: "I'm doing fine." Mom's view: " He's failing everywhere."), we met alone. He said that he wasn't good at talking, but I should see his girlfriend; she never stopped. I took him up on the offer and observed his passivity and disconnection with her. He smiled at us with his goofy grin and contributed as little as possible to the discussion. Testing supported what I had already surmised: that he was getting high several times a week, was mildly depressed, angry, and had significant feelings of inadequacy.

After considering the evidence, I realized that if I insisted on setting the priorities for therapy, I might as well cancel the next appointment. So I quickly put the authority in his hands. We had to meet regularly if he wanted to live at home (as his parents had stated) but, once he showed up, the plan was his (and even this was a choice we discussed. Some oppositional teenagers don't want to live at home and, when it's possible, I make alternative arrangements with them and their parents. Seth was not interested in having a harder life and opted quickly for staying at home). In therapy, we could talk, take walks, play games, do projects, eat, play on the computer—whatever he wanted. He opted for checkers, endless games of checkers. It doesn't matter that checkers is an activity for younger kids, since in no-talk therapy I care more about the developmental stage than the chronological age. Thus, Seth's attraction to a board game provided important information about his level of social maturity. He played with focus and determination, though, and often won. He was always a bit more connected after he had me surrounded. His smile wasn't so silly; he even seemed to like being with me as he acquired king after king.

I used brief interludes while setting up the board to get him to think with similar intensity about the moves he had been making at home and school. (I set up board games in slow motion; I also shuffle cards extensively to buy time to chat with no-talk kids.) I settled on a few messages that I attempted to communicate each time. It was his life and he had choices to make about how he would use it. This was not a dress rehearsal for some eventual performance, although he could certainly screw up and try again. But he needed to acknowledge that he had choices to make—and, no matter what he said, his behavior demonstrated those choices. Seth knew I liked him and looked forward to being with him. I agreed that his parents had way too many expectations for him, but when we got them to back off he had to show us he was really managing his life as a young adult.

Seth had few areas of success, though he enjoyed skateboarding and snowboarding and stayed quite busy. He wasn't particularly serious or ambitious about anything he did and tended to smoke pot and fool around with like-minded pals. He saw himself as fairly competent socially, but preferred to be with younger kids. In Seth's case, I was stumped for several weeks about how to improve his experience of success beyond trouncing me at checkers. My insight came at an unlikely time. We had an emergency family session when grades came out, and his parents produced his horrendous report card filled with D's and F's.

On this dismal page, a single grade of A stood out in dramatic relief: Seth, it turned out, was a great baker, and he had earned this excellent mark in his cooking class. The teacher had even written "cheerful and cooperative, doing fine work." We used the next session to call caterers and country clubs, hotels and restaurants, finding out about job openings. In keeping with the spirit of checkers, we took turns—dialing and speaking on the phone. Happily, the busy country-club season was approaching and one club he contacted had positions they would need to fill, assisting with the poolside grill. Seth was skeptical but made another call, filled out the forms, and interviewed successfully. He then began a meteoric career there. He worked first in the grill, then in the casual restaurant, then in the fancy one, helping to cater functions over the course of his senior year. Subsequently, with encouragement from his boss, he applied to culinary school.

Several months into treatment, meeting less frequently be-

cause of his work schedule, we continued to play checkers. After
a particularly stunning set of defeats for me, Seth looked up at
me with actual sympathy on his face. He asked, "How about I
give you some pointers here?" When I eventually won a round,
he gave *me* high fives, my proud instructor.

He never spoke to me in therapy about his problems. Long
after he won the last checkers game, he held to his position that
he put no stock in therapy. He wanted to be in charge of his
own life and viewed self-disclosure with utter mistrust to the
end. But, even so, he changed. His grades became merely atro-
cious, and he graduated from high school. He developed friendships with kids his own age and held down the cooking jobs for
the whole year I knew him. His parents followed through on my
suggestion to keep major expectations to a minimum, so there
were fewer conflicts at home, and he became more tolerable to
be around. He was less angry—even *letting* me beat him at
checkers once in a while, out of pity.

The notion of power in child therapy is critical to consider,
and quite complex. In general, no-talk kids, particularly the
overtly oppositional ones, tend to be hypersensitive to adult
control. By contrast, many verbal kids actually feel empowered
by therapy, since they want people to hear their stories. For
some talkative children and adolescents, the therapist may be
the first adult in their lives who has really listened to them.
They are able to use the rules and expectations of treatment to
their benefit. Even younger kids who have play skills may leave
sessions feeling stronger for all the attention paid to what matters to them.

But kids who enter treatment as part of a long line of relentless demands and criticisms find it almost entirely diminishing. If
we let them set the agenda, no matter how untherapeutic it appears to be, we begin to correct their skewed experiences of
adults and relationships *with* adults. Thus, even without describing the problem, we can begin to ameliorate it by attending
closely to the child with the problem.

Feeling Trapped

Some kids don't talk in therapy because they suspect or know that the consequences could be severe. Abused and unwanted kids, children of acrimonious divorces, those living with alcoholic or mentally ill parents, and survivors of trauma all know the value of silence and the costs of talking. Kids as young as three can intuit this rule for survival. Some kids come to therapy and show how cornered they are by actually sitting in a corner. Direct questioning will arouse anxiety and even panic. Kids who are cornered into silence require a kinder and gentler therapy, if they dare make use of therapy at all.

Paula, the 10-year-old who resided with her father and paternal grandmother (see p. 116), did not begin treatment as a no-talk kid. Through several miscalculations of mine, and the press of her real life, she turned into one. My assessment and treatment began in quite the standard fashion; we played, I met with the concerned adults, I visited the school, had a meeting with her father and teacher, called her mother on the phone, collected lots of background information, and we began, or so I thought, to lay the foundation for development of better negotiation and self-comforting skills, while I provided parent education and support.

But the situation outside my office kept escalating. Paula's father lost his job and started drinking. Her grandmother's diabetes got out of control and she blamed Paula for her high blood sugar. Paula's sympathetic teacher went on maternity leave, replaced by an inexperienced substitute who publicly criticized Paula's hair-twirling, thumb-sucking, and occasional urinary accidents. Hostility from all quarters was displaced onto this little girl, and any time I met with the adults they only wanted me to hear about all the horrible, destructive things she had done. She had taken Grandma's make-up and ruined it, she had cut the cat's fur, she had written on the walls in her room, she had totaled her bicycle, she had set fire to tissues in the bathroom and almost burned down the apartment. School meetings were almost as ugly; she didn't do her homework, she had no friends, she smelled, she was disruptive, she didn't take her coat off, she wouldn't stop sucking her thumb. Reinforcing behavioral strategies didn't work—because Paula was in increasing distress emotionally, and because *no one* was able to sustain positive changes.

I began to meet with Paula alone, first to reestablish trust, and then to strategize with her about what she needed from the family sessions. She had some interesting complaints, mostly about wanting more attention from her father and grandmother. When she behaved well, they left her alone. Thus, she had figured out a multitude of methods for getting the only kind of response they seemed capable of.

I called her father before a scheduled family session and described to him the simple goal of the meeting: to establish a time he and his mother would play with Paula in the following week. I told him that we would not be diverted from this agenda and that I would be helping Paula speak for herself. While this was a very minor triumph in light of the general harshness of Paula's life, this session did provide her with the rare taste of advocacy that she so desperately needed. And, at the next appointment, she proudly brought in some cookies she had made with her grandmother, along with a huge smile.

But this intervention was utterly inadequate as a response to the profound toxicity in Paula's environment. Several months into therapy, I discovered several dismaying facts: (1) I was being used as punishment, as in, "we'll see what your therapist has to say about this"; (2) as part of this hostile circle of adults, there was little I could *say* that could support Paula in any useful way; and (3) as her play became more disorganized and fragmented, and as she related less and less about her home life, I was tacitly contributing to the very downward spiral I was being paid to prevent. By behaving in kindly but ultimately unhelpful ways, I was, in fact, making her life worse.

While I was unwilling to give up my relationship with Paula because I cared about her, and she had so few adults who did, I woke up to the fact that I wasn't contributing much on my own. I scratched my treatment plan and called on the wraparound team: representatives from many different agencies around town—school, social services, respite care, home-based services, family members, her pediatrician, and several other therapists who worked with multiproblem families. After we convened, and once many other professionals were on board, I cut my treatment back to once a month and let an intensive home-based family team do their work. I also helped Paula get a scholarship to the local Y after-school program, so she was at home less and having a bit more fun. Her father got respite care and support finding a new job. These multisystemic interventions helped for a time. In fact, when her father pulled her from therapy because he thought the family had enough people involved, I even felt hopeful, knowing a fine circle of adults was surrounding the family.

But Paula's story does not end so happily and serves as a kind of sobering reminder about the limitations of what we have to offer some kids. At age 12, Paula began hanging around with her father's short-wave CB radio buddies, many in their twenties and thirties. While there was no evidence that her father had ever sexually abused Paula, he often included her in his adult social activities, and she was clearly vulnerable to mistreatment by this group of men. Yet the local child protection agency had long ago closed the case and was not interested in reopening it without an actual report of abuse.

However, it wasn't really a surprise when Paula became pregnant shortly after her 13th birthday. She was moved to a group home for the last part of her pregnancy and then stayed there with her infant; however, she was unable to comply with the home's expectations—designed, as they were, for older adolescent girls. She was "written up" for leaving dirty diapers around, for handling her son roughly, and for being inattentive to him. Her baby was placed in foster care and she was, concurrently, moved to another group residence.

Because hindsight is 20-20, I can safely say that I should have convened the circle of adults immediately and refused to do family therapy with such hostile parents. But even with as much support as a community can summon, some no-talk kids do not become more connected and resilient; for them interventions have little or no beneficial effect. They may have families that are overwhelmed by their own traumatic histories, and have insufficient resources and skills. The loss of a safe, supported childhood wears them down and, especially when the troubled environment is compounded by physical or sexual abuse, the relentless onslaught to their self-esteem takes its toll.

Thus, kids who are trapped in a corner before and during treatment may require some extraordinary interventions. We'll have to consider all possibilities of help, including out-of-home crisis placement. These extremely high-risk kids pose unusual treatment challenges. They need therapists who are stubborn, determined, and tenacious (cf. Kagan, 1996). Often, therapy and a multisystemic circle of adults engaged over an extended period of time *can* help stabilize these desperate kids.

Shyness

Shy kids pose particular kinds of challenges for therapy. Parents often hope that therapy will correct the "problem" of shyness. This desire is also frequently shared by the shy child or adolescent. We are asked to assist in the child's transformation from anxious, or socially phobic, into confident, outspoken, and outgoing. Facing such expectations, we need to set the record straight right away—and promise no such thing. "Shy" describes a wide variety of kids. Some are more timid in large social situations but confident in small groups. A few become *increasingly* withdrawn over the years and express extreme misery about the ordinary social demands of life. Most learn, on their own, to cover up their embarrassment and get on with their lives. However, even though we may be able to add a few coping skills to their strategies for managing, shy kids will not suddenly snap out of it, no matter how brilliant the intervention.

The very act of speaking in therapy arouses a certain degree of panic for children and adolescents who are shy. If we press them to speak to us, we can make them feel worse instead of better. These kids need to be distracted from their plight, and then taught how to focus their attention elsewhere. While developing their empathic sense to perceive that other people are also self-conscious and self-doubting, we may even help them *pretend* not to be shy to get through time-limited demand situations. All the while, though, we have an obligation to honor their wiring. We cannot change the essence of who they are.

Amanda, the 11-year-old, agonizingly shy child (see p. 117), shared her parents' desire for her to be able to assert herself more effectively. She wasn't doing well in school because she rarely got up the nerve to participate in group discussions, and she absolutely refused to stand up in front of the class for oral reports. She had few friends because she would freeze when people approached her. Her inability to speak up for herself had serious implications that could lead to others' taking advantage of her. Already, her mother had noted that Amanda was going along with the wrong crowd at school. At the same time, she had a loving and supportive family and was a member of a successful swim team. Importantly, despite the problem for which she was referred for treatment, she already had some notable success in her life. In Amanda's case, the assessment period was brief; it was apparent that all involved shared the same explanation for the referral, including me.

Amanda came to the first session trembling. Each question I asked turned her face ablaze. After about five minutes, I realized that this one-on-one conversation was incredibly tough for her, and so I quickly moved to some diversionary tactics. I suggested we make some puppets who could then have their own conversation in a couple of weeks. I brought out a bag of scraps, googly eyes, old socks, and felt, and we set to work, side by side. We occasionally stopped to admire the other's handiwork or to address the sew-it-or-glue-it question that plagues all puppet makers. Otherwise, we spent that hour, and another the following week, in amiable silence, producing a half-dozen wacky alter egos.

As a silly puppet, Amanda was significantly less retiring. She had some shockingly strong things to say with her fanged-wolf voice and was compellingly frightened as a little rabbit. The main point, though, is that she was able to develop many strong voices that she had not used before. Without ever discussing her paralyzing shyness, Amanda was beginning to talk (albeit mostly in the high squeaky voice of baby puppet animals.)

Over a couple of months, we used our puppets, play telephones, and even e-mail to talk about the aspects of shyness that Amanda disliked the most. In all these modes, we practiced the fine art of distinguishing the different voices she had within her. Together, we worked to develop a more daring persona who could make play dates and talk in class. Amanda worked on shifting into the acting mode, and called her persona Elaine after a brassy TV character she liked. To stop thinking about her anxiety, she worked to focus on some external object, to consider how others might be feeling, and to do "Elaine." Throughout our time together, I underscored the point that shyness, like hair color or the lovely arches in her feet, was just one characteristic of who she was.

No-talk therapy works with shy kids because it avoids their weaknesses and fears. Instead of calling attention to them through scrutiny and invasive questions, focus is diverted onto a joint activity. Instead of getting them to change in some essential way, it establishes that we will instead work to honor who they are, while developing new skills. And, through the empathic connection of the therapeutic relationship, it moves them away from the excruciating and exclusive focus on their internal states, to how other people might be feeling and what else is going on in the room. Finally, in no-talk therapy, shy kids use fun and fantasy to call upon stronger and more vocal parts of themselves that can speak up as needed in particular situations.

Disengagement

Of all the kinds of no-talk kids we work with, disengaged and apathetic children are certainly among the most difficult. Often,

these kids are referred as part of a diversionary strategy to keep
them out of the juvenile justice system. Even the very young
antisocial kids we see may appear headed down that road if we
can't intervene effectively. They usually have stories that are depressing both for what has been done to them and for what, in
turn, they have done. The cycle of violence is unbroken. And
these narratives are especially concerning in light of significant
data suggesting that most aggressive criminal behavior can be
predicted by the time a child is four years old (Karr-Morse &
Wiley, 1998). Untreated antisocial children do indeed grow up
to become dangerous adults.

Many disengaged kids have had to cope with extreme emotional as well as physical trauma. Like other noncompliant children, they have developed an array of maladaptive strategies for
keeping human connection to a minimum. But they take it a step
farther. Whereas defiant children are continuously offering a
challenge to *someone*, disengaged kids demonstrate a kind of
hopelessness about anyone being there at all. They act impul-
sively or destructively, out of internal needs or beliefs, without
regard for what others might think or do.

Martin, the disengaged 14-year-old boy (see p. 119), was initially chilling to be around. He would mumble and stare with
vacant eyes. He made messes and sneered if I commented on
them. He came in stoned the third time we met and sauntered
out when I banished him. He returned a couple of weeks later
and sighed with terminal ennui when I attempted to discuss my
rules about attending therapy straight (I have a need to be
treated differently from a video game). He gave nothing back,
would not talk, would not play, would not listen. He was a clock
watcher, but killed the time efficiently ripping off the cuff
threads on his jeans, one strand at a time, with the diligence of a
neurosurgeon. He wanted to be left to his own devices and forgotten, and was often successful at achieving this. Even his
mother, as worried as she was, failed to bring him to a couple of
appointments.

I met with the school counselor who referred him, and spoke

with two of his previous therapists. I also visited his home to try to get a fuller sense of who he was. Martin lived in the country, on a farm, where he tended pigs, chickens and horses. Although his mother had to remind him frequently to go to the barn, she noted that once out there he spent many hours after his chores, just patting the animals and talking softly to them. I received this information with enormous hope; tenderness toward animals is a remarkable accomplishment for a child this furious and depressed. On my home visit, I got to see this side of Martin. Summoning up the image of him nuzzling nose to nose with his horse helped me to stay optimistic.

Martin's life was a mess. It was tough to find a way in. I was unwilling to ask about school, pot-smoking or how he was getting along with his parents. Such questions did nothing to help him feel better or act better; in fact, they had the opposite effect and alienated him from therapy and from me all the more. My approach took Martin's mother a long time to accept. She often threatened to pull him from treatment if I didn't "make him talk" about these significant problems (and she did terminate before I felt we were done). But in my mind he lacked the success and skill to negotiate about his choices. I resolved to help him build some competencies before pursuing the details of his mismanaged life.

I cast about for successes. At first, I wondered if his guitar playing could be developed, but he was adamant that he didn't want to play with anyone, or for anyone, or take lessons. He took pleasure only in sitting in his room and playing loud dissonant chords modeled after his deceased idol, Kurt Cobain. After a month I had exhausted my supply of fun strategies that might provide a connection, however tenuous. Several crisis calls from the school, saying he had been truant most of the week and fallen asleep in class when he finally returned, gave me further indication that I needed to act quickly.

I gave his mother the name of a child psychiatrist for a possible prescription for antidepressant medication. He had been self-medicating with marijuana, and continued use would interfere with the effectiveness of real medicine, but Martin clearly still needed such an evaluation. Then, in my pursuit of a bit of success, knowing he wouldn't be able to tolerate too much social contact, I had his mother call the veterinarians in town, hoping to find one interested in hiring a surly assistant dog walker and cage cleaner.

A kindly older vet agreed to take Martin on as an "apprentice," and Martin agreed to go to meet him and observe some surgery that was scheduled. The next session, for the first time, Martin spoke to me in full sentences, describing (in almost too much detail) the spaying of a Bernese Mountain Dog and the declawing of a cat.

Over the next two months, Martin began to change. He talked more in therapy about his work at the vet's and about other interests, particularly death. He attended school more regularly since he could not otherwise work at the vet's. And with antidepressants on board he seemed less dour and disconnected and more aware of his surroundings.

Therapy with Martin never became easy. Nor did it focus on the problems of antisocial acting-out that had gotten him there in the first place. But his life was not easy, either. His parents detested each other, and neither was available to him. They both abused alcohol and marijuana, so their stated concerns about his pot-smoking didn't convince anyone. His mother was also prone to violent, rageful fits that were senseless to Martin and actually made it wise for him to hide out in his room.

My major goal, getting Martin to see himself as a boy with a future, seemed increasingly attainable over the time we worked together. His attendance and focus in school improved, and he seemed less depressed and isolated. And, while we never spoke in much detail about his problems, he was evidently intrigued by being with an adult who listened as hard as I tried to. He'd respond to my questions with surprise, saying, "You want to know *that?*" He even made some efforts, as the weeks passed, to tell me about the weird and dark world he inhabited.

Martin's mother had unresolved anguish of her own and didn't want to come to family sessions or make time for her own healing. Nor did she want her son attaching to someone else. Aware of this tension, I was sad but not surprised when she called to say she couldn't rearrange her work to bring him in anymore. I was hopeful, though, that the tenuous connections he had made to me and to his work at the vet's would make a difference for him down the road.

Therapy with disengaged kids is both humbling and grounding. These children and adolescents test our theories and techniques until we question what we could possibly offer them given the reality of their lives. They sit across from us and it can feel as though they are on the other side of the Sahara. At the beginning, we don't know if we can become an oasis for them— or if we will remain just another mirage. Given the instability of their environments, we can never be certain how much time we'll have to establish and deepen a therapeutic connection. Thus, we work harder to facilitate "something to be proud of." They may at least be able to keep some success in their lives, even when they no longer have us.

The therapy of realistic hope keeps, at its foundation, the glimmer of possiblility. We remain cautiously optimistic that we can build a healing relationship, can find areas of success, can enhance self-esteem, can make a difference. Sometimes, hope is all we have, but even the most hardened child desperately needs us to keep it alive.

9

No-Talk Therapy: Terminable and Interminable

AT SOME POINT, THERAPY ends, but no-talk stories can have unpredictable conclusions. We may find ourselves in the midst of a work of flash fiction (over after a session or two) or a multigenerational saga (years of treatment). And, since we tailor no-talk therapy to each particular child or adolescent, it should not surprise us that the endings we develop (or encounter) say something important about the specific relationship story we have told. For many kids who have never had the luxury of saying "good-bye" to someone they cared for, the ending of treatment can be as therapeutic as all the work that preceded it.

We may find ourselves struggling to get kids into therapy and losing them long before we have been helpful—or, conversely, feeling we're done with a phase of work but staying involved anyway, albeit more peripherally. When we talk about termination, then, we are describing endings that can go according to plan, or require modification, or are downright bombs. Some no-talk kids stay through a proper termination, but many drop out and more than a few do both—arriving and departing several times over the years.

BEST ENDINGS

There is widespread consensus in the child therapy literature that termination should occur when the treatment objectives are met, not before or after. While we try to keep kids hanging in through "flights into health" and insurance hassles, we also need to be clear that we'll never fix everything and that we can do "enough." If kids are connecting as well as they can, have some areas of developmental success, and some self-soothing and problem-solving skills, it's time to wind down.

All types of therapy have stated goals, of course, and these describe when it is time to end. In some more solution-focused methods, termination is dictated by the resolution of a presenting problem; the more analytic approaches, on the other hand, may have deeper developmental purposes. With the exception of the psychoanalytic literature, however, the *process* of termination hasn't received extensive study.

In a review of studies giving reasons for termination of child therapy, Brems (1993, p. 399) offers a fairly complete list, summarized from reports by a wide range of clinicians:

- resolution of presenting problems
- reduction or disappearance of symptoms
- developmentally appropriate cognitions
- developmentally appropriate expressions of affect
- developmentally appropriate experiences of affect
- developmentally appropriate morality
- developmentally appropriate self-development
- developmentally appropriate interpersonal relationships
- increased problem-solving ability
- increased cognitive flexibility
- ability to generalize and adapt skills to new situations

- better coping ability
- increased spontaneity in behavior
- increased spontaneity in affect expression
- increased spontaneity in need expression
- greater capacity for enjoyment
- increased self confidence
- increased self-esteem or self-value
- increasingly clear self-definition
- increased independence
- internalized ability to set limits and boundaries
- decreased experience of intrapsychic conflict
- decreased experience of interpersonal conflict
- decreased experience of familial conflict

Although this list is relatively comprehensive, the goals overlap and interconnect in intimate ways—for example, greater flexibility of thought tends to improve problem-solving, reduce interpersonal conflict, and enhance self-esteem. Working on one stated goal typically benefits other areas of development as well.

The goals of no-talk therapy are much more concrete but evolve over time into the accomplishment of these other objectives. For example, the fun that Seth had playing checkers with me led to increased self-confidence, increased problem-solving ability, and decreased experience of interpersonal conflict. However, our therapeutic planning never involves just the inner life of the no-talk kid. The goals for termination also need to describe the range of activities, people, and services that will remain central to the child and family long after therapy is a memory. Ideally, the whole circle of adults becomes invested in our work. The decision to terminate no-talk therapy is not made unilaterally; it includes the child's broader context. Optimally, treatment objectives in no-talk therapy are met when the child or adolescent:

- has important peer friendships
- participates in activities of interest and challenge
- has connections to a family, extended family, and community

- can identify and use sources of support provided by the circle of adults
- is achieving adequately in school
- is on the path to a future

PREMATURE AND UNPLANNED TERMINATIONS

In no-talk therapy, premature endings occur more frequently than optimal terminations. This isn't surprising; in child therapy in general, attrition rates range from approximately 30 to 70 percent (e.g., Kazdin, 1996; Novick, Benson, & Rembar, 1981). In a review of child treatment outcome studies, Weisz, Weiss, Alicke, and Klotz (1987) established that, on average, kids are in therapy for just 9.5 sessions. However, their findings support the idea that more intensive forms of treatment produce more beneficial effects. In light of these data, we should give priority to assessing the factors surrounding treatment dropout and to minimizing attrition. There are many reasons for kids to leave therapy, but we can draw no overwhelming conclusions from the available data.

It is even hard to find consensus among researchers and clinicians about what a therapy dropout is. Premature termination can be attributed to anticipated duration of treatment or to differing goals set by the therapist and the family. Families may "drop out" because the therapist hasn't met their expectations or has met enough of them. For no-talk kids, the distinction between attending and dropping out may be particularly vague, since they have the ability to attend sessions in body only. The different explanations for dropping out can be divided into child and family reasons, therapist reasons and environmental reasons.

Child and Family Reasons

Among the family factors cited as possible causes of dropping out, the most frequent include: moves; socioeconomic disadvantage; younger, single parents; degree of coercion in referral; delay in waiting for services; geographical distance from services and transportation problems; unsatisfactory history of previous treatment; parental stress, pathology, and substance abuse; parental history of antisocial behavior; unrealistic parental expectations and attitudes; and harsh and abusive parenting practices (e.g., Armbruster & Kazdin, 1994; Brems, 1993; Kazdin, 1996). In sum, all the kinds of families that have no-talk kids. But the findings regarding the relative impact of these factors on dropping out are contradictory and generally inconclusive (e.g., Armbruster & Kazdin, 1994). Parents also pull kids from treatment when they feel the situation has improved sufficiently or isn't improving quickly enough, or because they have other priorities. The family motivations for premature termination appear to be numerous.

Looking at these data, it is safe to say is that the kids who are dropping out tend to be those who are in the greatest distress (e.g., Kazdin, Mazurick, & Siegel, 1994). Dropping out is associated with a variety of child factors: more severe psychopathology and more diagnoses; severity of antisocial behavior; extent of school delay and problems; a marginal peer group; and a lack of attachment and connection (though the opposite can also be true—too great a fear of abandonment can also lead a child to terminate prematurely). Being a no-talk kid could in itself be somewhat predictive of dropping out of therapy, as well as of therapist-led termination. It should be of concern to child therapists that the increased need for treatment is somehow associated with the *increased* likelihood of dropping out.

Therapist Reasons

No-talk kids and their families aren't the only ones who can't stick with therapy until its natural conclusion. Graduate students and post-graduates often have cases that conclude with the academic year, whether or not termination is indicated. Therapists move around, too, and cope with burn-out in a variety of sometimes constructive, sometimes questionable ways that may mean ending according to *our* needs, and not because therapeutic goals have been met. We become ill, or pregnant, or take new jobs. Although it is sometimes unavoidable, when we instigate premature termination for these reasons, we are invariably undermining the collaborative nature of no-talk work. As Dewald (1980) has noted, for the child, therapist-initiated termination

> represents a unilateral decision made by someone else—a decision which does not take into account his or her own emotional or therapeutic needs. It may be perceived as a repetition of arbitrary, unexpected, and "selfish" behavior of early key figures particularly when there have been significant or traumatic separations earlier in the patient's life. (p. 14)

As must be said again, we can't establish a relationship with every no-talk kid who comes into the office. We may end prematurely with a kid because we don't like him, are frightened of him, can't figure out how to help him, or generally perceive a mismatch between us. We behave responsibly in these cases by making a referral to another person or program or by going back to the circle of adults for reconsideration.

But we have to attend to the process, no matter what our reasons for termination. We may feel sad, guilty, frustrated, and depressed. The stress in our lives that leads to the termination can cause us to withdraw emotionally and play our own kind of no-talk game—colluding with the child or adolescent to deny and minimize our importance to her. It's easier to think that a quick referral is all that's needed, to lay blame on the crazy parents, their unmotivated kids, the wrong developmental moment for therapy to begin. But, ultimately, if we need to end early, we're obligated to do our best to make sense of what this early termination means to the no-talk kid and to us, and to make treatment more successful somewhere else.

Environmental Reasons

Kids in toxic environments have trouble sustaining a therapeutic relationship because their survival doesn't immediately depend on it. They need to be persuaded that treatment can make a difference in their lives because they're wary of relationships and have a right to be skeptical. But the community mental health system that was designed to help these kids is overburdened; its clinicians are treating more damaged kids, for shorter periods, and with fewer innovations. And only a small fraction of families who need treatment are receiving it. Our strategies for getting multiproblem families into treatment and providing them with the supports they'll need to keep coming haven't worked well, and there is no evidence that more resources will be forthcoming. Even if kids do get into the community mental health system, they don't usually stay until problems are resolved. The child-attrition rates in these agencies, at the upper end of all studies, speak to this difficulty.

Another environmental reason for premature termination is managed care. The move of insurance companies towards controlling access to mental health is not based *in any way* on what we know about child development, trauma, attachment, and healing. It also means that therapists are often managing their treatment plans instead of directly serving clients. The amount of time spent on the phone and in meetings is already significant in child therapy; in some complex cases the amount of collateral time spent actually exceeds face-to-face contact with a child. The managed care component can make it nearly impossible for us to do what we need to do to reach damaged and disconnected kids. Under unrealistic time pressure, benefits often dry up before goals are met. Too often, we have to fit the treatment to the number of sessions and not to the individual child or adolescent, even when this makes little clinical or ethical sense.

Conflict in the circle of adults can also lead to premature termination. Turf wars, divergent goals, changes in personnel, and personality conflicts can all undermine the efficacy of no-talk therapy. This work is hard, takes *time*, and is made tougher by many factors in the environment that can operate against our efforts.

AVOIDING PREMATURE TERMINATION

Because the consequences of premature termination are serious, we need to figure out what we can do to keep no-talk kids engaged. Interestingly, in his review of the attrition prevention literature, Kazdin (1996) sounds like a no-talk therapist: ". . . the notion of therapeutic alliance deserves greater attention. . . . Development of the alliance may have important implications for attrition in child and adolescent therapy" (p. 151). He notes that the alliance between parents and the therapist is also probably important. Even without powerful supporting data, this point seems quite obvious clinically. And such an alliance is, of course, the bread and butter of no-talk therapy.

Kazdin (1996) also concluded that the expectations that parents and children bring to treatment may shed light on premature termination. He concludes that families are more likely to remain in therapy when their expectations are congruent with the services provided. Thus, the mutual goal-setting early in no-talk therapy serves as a buffer against premature termination. We need to remain clear with children, parents, and all others involved about who we are in the circle and what it is we plan to accomplish. Expectations also encompass belief about the nature, cause, and course of clinical problems and the appropriate focus of treatment. Expectations that are incongruent with the therapy provided are related to dropping out, according to several studies (e.g., Kazdin, Mazurick, & Siegel, 1994; Plunkett, 1984). Thus, "getting on the same page" with everyone early on may retain the involvement of families who might otherwise drop out.

Other promising treatment data suggest that families who receive needed supports beyond therapy also stay engaged more effectively. It seems logical that we need to alleviate parental stressors rather than compound them; Kazdin (1996) refers to this as a "burden of treatment model" (p. 140). It is likely that some families who drop out of treatment have so many sources of stress in their lives that participating in therapy actually makes matters worse. For example, getting to sessions can involve logistics and transportation, cajoling an unwilling child, siblings, and spouse, arranging babysitting, the financial stress of paying therapy bills or co-payments, and the many demands of treatment (e.g., "homework assignments," behavioral contracts, more school meetings). Happily, no-talk therapy also addresses this through the circle of adults; we seek to support the whole family, not just the child.

AVOIDING EXCESSIVE THERAPY

When we are successful establishing an alliance and becoming an important adult in a no-talk kid's life, we sometimes wonder how to terminate "the right way." Our own countertransference, the neediness of the child and family, and the centrality of our participation in the circle of adults—all this can make us hang in beyond the point of therapeutic benefit.

The love that we develop for kids and our own investment in the relationship with them can make it harder for us to plan to say goodbye. With wounded children, we'll never be able to resolve all the struggles of their lives, nor to ensure their complete safety. As tough as it can be for *us* to accept, we won't always be there for them. And, as powerful as the relationship is, we need to know that it is also a model for other connections and to help the child develop those, too. We must never think of ourselves as irreplaceable, as the only one who can help. This is a trap that will make termination impossible. And, as we all know, the therapeutic relationship has an end built into it from the beginning.

Kids may come to feel these same powerful emotions toward us and not want treatment to end, either. Their parents, similarly, may find our support essential. Sometimes, we try to minimize our importance to kids—the briefer and cognitive-behavioral treatments don't even address termination. The implication is that we can just do some therapeutic things, shake hands, and get out. Gillman (1991) uses the term "childism" to describe this tendency to avoid the therapist's enormous significance for the child through nonpsychoanalytic psychotherapy. He notes that "childism" results from "ignorance, countertransference, and the child's relative inability to verbalize his feelings" (p. 340). If kids don't say how much we mean to them, we may feel safe in assuming that the technique has been more significant than the relationship. But, even in brief, solution-focused work with children, they *are* attending to how they feel being with us.

Our participation in the circle of adults can also confuse the decision to terminate. When so many people have a say, developing consensus can become a less than clinical decision. As we plan our obsolescence we'll need to make sure that natural supports in the community can pick up where we leave off. We have to refer to our goals, as well as the evolution of the therapeutic relationship, to make our termination plans, even if others in the circle of adults beg us to remain central players. (Since we may stay involved in a peripheral way, we can offer some consultation services even after we stop regular treatment.)

TYPES OF NO-TALK ENDINGS

If the relationship with kids is primary in no-talk therapy, then it follows that how we say goodbye will have vital importance to them. We need to find the method and style of ending our work that fits for a particular child or adolescent. In optimal circumstances, when, together with the child, we determine the length and content of the treatment, we are limited only by the bounds of our creativity. No-talk terminations include all of the following strategies, and perhaps many others.

Commencements

The choice of the word "termination" can be particularly irksome when it is applied to work with kids; it suggests an ignorance of attachment theory and child development. Furthermore, thanks to Hollywood's endless supply of violent action films, it suggests more grisly finality than just the end of a relationship. A better word choice might be "commencement" or "graduation." We can have commencement ceremonies that symbolize completion of a phase of therapy without implying anything so dire as death or abandonment. From firsthand experience we can explain that people who graduate at one point in their lives can always return for more advanced study at another. Devising a commencement ceremony that fits a particular relationship honors both the child's accomplishments and the therapeutic relationship itself.

A commencement or graduation ceremony usually takes a couple weeks of planning, once we have decided that it will be the farewell method of choice. While it need not be so complex as to require an engraved program, the child's style and interest should be paramount. Some ceremonies *are* quite elaborate, and include speeches, an audience (e.g., the family, the circle of adults, other therapists), photos, gift exchanges, and even a reception (e.g., lemonade and cupcakes). Other comencements are simpler: We say something about the experience and ask the child and the other adults if they'd like to do so as well. We may invite the involved adults to a presentation or performance, go out for a meal, or have an ice cream party—anything that acknowledges a job well done. In all commencements, a diploma is essential; one can easily be made on a computer.

As with most important transitions in a child's life, graduation elicits mixed emotions. According to their emotional maturity, kids will be able to grasp that they may be having some complicated feelings: excited and worried; proud and sad; confident and nostalgic. Our job at commencement, then, is to give voice to the different emotional aspects of graduation, emphasizing at once the inherent internal conflict between feelings of success and of loss. But we should also be inclusive, giving the child *and* ourselves permission to be both proud *and* sad at the same time.

Rites of Passage

Like graduations, rites of passage offer a chance to celebrate and honor a developmental milestone. However, they are designed to consolidate the child's transition to a new identity: from victim to survivor, from failure to success, from inept to expert. Such rites of passage provide a distinct metaphor for the ending of therapy—viewing it not as a termination but a celebration of the child's new status.

In most cultures, and for most kids, growing up involves a series of rites of passage. From birthdays and confirmations to bar mitzvahs and driver's licenses, kids look forward to the next milestone that highlights their growth. But it is quite typical for no-talk kids, especially traumatized and alienated ones, to have had little positive experience with being at center stage in this way. Thus, rites of passage take on extra meaning for them, providing a particularly potent way to say goodbye.

Epston and White (1992, 1995) use rites of passage to end narrative therapy with children and adolescents. Their strategies are readily adaptable for some no-talk kids. When Epston and White terminate a course of treatment, they conduct a series of interviews in which they elicit and document a child's "alternative knowledges." Once a child has mastered her particular difficulties, she then gives an interview describing her achievements and experiences. This rite of passage conveys to kids that they are authorities on their own lives, that what they know and can do is worthy of respect, and that their ideas are significant enough to be documented and circulated to others. In this vein, Epston and White (1992) describe how rites of passage enable kids to:

> . . . negotiate the passage from novice to veteran, from client to consultant. Rather than instituting a dependency on the "expert knowledge" presented by the therapist and other authorities, this therapy enables persons to arrive at a point where they can take

recourse to liberating alternatives and "special" knowledges that
they have resurrected and/or generated during therapy. (p. 280)

The rite of passage doesn't have to be an extensive interview.
But it should give children the pleasure of "show and tell," so
they can exhibit their self-knowledge and share it with others.
Through a display of projects, a book compiling accomplishments, letters, a puppet show, a psychodrama, handbooks, certificates, artwork, a taped interview, or another symbolic gesture,
the rite of passage conveys to the child that he has accomplished something significant.

For some children and adolescents, the most important aspect
of the rite of passage is being able to provide expertise to other
kids who have not yet mastered similar problems. They become
resources to peers just beginning therapy, either through direct
consultation or through written material they help produce. For
instance, they can write letters or books about what they have
learned and give permission for these to be used by the therapist
(e.g., Freeman et al., 1997). Occasionally, therapy graduates
even agree to participate in public speaking, for example, talking
to teachers and parents about their learning disability.

Open-door Terminations

In an "open-door termination," the child has not necessarily
completed therapy, but has done enough work to resolve the
most pressing matters in his life for the time being. Both the
therapist and the child know that they may meet again in a few
months, or even a few years, as new issues crop up or new cognitive ability permits a revised understanding of the past.

With many no-talk kids whose attachment histories are troubled, we are particularly reluctant to sever an intense, meaningful relationship—one that may be the first such connection
they've been able to sustain. While keeping a hand outreached,
we acknowledge that they have "done a chunk of work" and let
them know they can return whenever they need to. Open-door

terminations are particularly helpful for emotionally needy kids who truly come to enjoy time with us and view ending therapy as punishment, no matter how rewarding we make it sound. Knowing they can come back gives them sufficient control to consider saying "goodbye for now."

In her work with traumatized kids, Beverly James (1989) typically approaches termination with an open-door policy. She notes:

> The youngsters are taught from the beginning that their work, with the help of the therapist, is to understand and accept what has happened to them, and to work on possible related problems, and that, when that is completed, a phase of treatment is over. The children learn that their relationship with the clinician changes, but does not necessarily end. (p. 177)

The truth is, of course, that many children do return for treatment. The open-door termination may be a realistic way of pausing treatment for the majority of no-talk kids who will reexperience the legacy of trauma at different developmental stages and need therapy again.

Vacations

While open-door terminations leave the return to treatment entirely up to the child and family, vacations from therapy provide the certainty of resumption. Some kids do well with an intermittent model of treatment that can be hard to define: Is it long-term therapy, practiced in fits and starts, or is it repeated efforts at brief intervention? One way of viewing work that proceeds in pulses is to consider the benefit of frequent and extended vacations for work of any kind. We are most productive when we are rested, and are more willing to put in an effort when we know we'll have a break in the future.

For kids who both crave and fear intimate relationships, a model incorporating long vacations works especially well. Once

a connection is established, some no-talk kids thrive on a hand-
ful of visits every few months. Then they go off to practice what
they've learned. It's as much intensity as they can stand. This
approach to not-ending suits their need to have important people remain in their lives, as well as their ambivalence about it.
Some kids with attachment disorder, for example, may need to
have enduring, though not necessarily frequent, treatment.

Similarly, kids who come from violent and socially toxic environments, have families with persisting significant dysfunction,
are part of the foster-care system, or have developmental disabilities or other difficulties that won't resolve quickly may benefit
from ongoing therapy with long vacations. As Byrne (1997) has
noted in her discussion of families that return repeatedly to family treatment: "We should not be too quick to call those who
return 'recidivist' or those who stay 'cooperative'. . . . Satisfaction
may involve leaving and returning" (p. 174). For no-talk kids and
their families, this support over an extended period of time can
lead to both satisfaction and healing.

Family Practice Model

Another model for "termination" of no-talk therapy is taken directly from family medicine, where a yearly check-up is routine.
As with the family physician, a relationship with the therapist is
maintained over time, but not necessarily actively. We may be
called upon occasionally by the parents for a phone consultation, or may provide regular, useful checkups, or may give the
child a needed clinical "booster shot" during another developmental phase.

In the family practice model, we do end a course of treatment. However, at the point of termination of regular therapy,
we establish a time in the future for a follow-up appointment.
We say goodbye the way a medical practioner might, fully expecting to see the child and family at their next check-up, whenever that may be.

Planned Endings

While many no-talk kids benefit from the varieties of "interminable" treatment, some really require that we set a time and a date for ending therapy and stick to it, just as prescribed by the more traditional schools of therapy. Also, for some children and adolescents, the idea of graduation or a rite of passage may represent a watering-down of the intensity of the termination process. Planned endings pay close attention to issues of separation, loss, and mourning, as well as, of course, achievements.

In a completed therapy, a child may experience the whole gamut of social experience, from initial attachment to ultimate loss. A successful ending to treatment teaches children how to say goodbye to someone important to them without feeling overwhelmed, abandoned, alone, or rejected. It is presumptuous of us to assume we'll always be there; the ending in psychotherapy *is* just one of the many losses these kids will experience throughout their lives.

With planned endings, we take the last few weeks of treatment to think about how saying goodbye affects a particular child. We prepare her for termination by finishing projects, talking about losses, and thinking about the ways that people move on in their lives. Without our help, she may be inclined to deal with these hard feelings by minimizing the meaning of the connection and repressing her genuine competence to handle separation. Sadly, this may then become the model she'll use to cope with future departures and losses. As an important element in some treatments, then, the skills acquired through termination are as vital as any others developed over the preceding months.

Endings in the Mail

As discussed earlier, no-talk kids lead unpredictable lives. Sometimes we don't get to establish any kind of termination plan. The child or adolescent simply disappears. He may miss an unreason-

able number of appointments, call and say he's no longer coming, move too far away, or be whisked off into a more restrictive
treatment setting. The thread of connection is severed without
any celebration or acknowledgment. For many kids, this arbi-
trary and meaningless loss of a relationship is par for the course,
no different from what they have come to expect.

When kids leave therapy prematurely, we can write them a
letter saying goodbye, reviewing all of their accomplishments,
discussing what they meant to us, and emphasizing what we
learned from them. If they had a project they were completing,
we may send it along, with the necessary materials to finish up.
If they write back, we'll keep it going—and have the corre-
spondence serve as the termination "visits." The most important
aspect of ending in the mail is that we don't allow the relationship to evaporate unacknowledged. Down the line, we may find
out that kids we hardly knew have saved our cards and notes as
they have moved around.

Passing the Torch

In therapy with families, a child is often the symptom-bearer for
struggles that are occurring in the family system and in other
family members. Through distressed and distressing behavior,
the no-talk kid gets himself and his family into therapy. From
here, the child makes improvements and settles down. At the
point we're terminating work with a particular child, our attention may be drawn inexorably toward a parent, a marriage, a
sibling, or a whole system in dramatic need of a tune-up.

The passing of the torch is common in no-talk therapy, and
includes a variety of scenarios. These tend to evolve when the
no-talk kid has begun to have a confident voice, at least some of
the time. For example:

- The no-talk kid won't talk in individual therapy but has a lot
  to say to his parents. The torch is passed from the child-as-
  problem to family-communication-as-problem.

- The no-talk kid does begin to talk—about the wife abuse in the home or her parents' impending divorce, for example. The torch is passed from child-as-problem to marital-distress-as-problem.
- The no-talk kid begins to have some success, and a sibling who has been overlooked becomes increasingly troubled. The torch is passed to the sibling.
- The no-talk kid is really managing adequately, but one of his parents is not—the parent is depressed, having an affair, abusing alcohol, or exhibiting some other serious difficulty. The torch is passed to a parent.

At this point in therapy, the contact with the family and the circle of adults shifts a bit but doesn't end. However, at this time we might thank the child or adolescent for getting help for the other family members. We'll note he has bravely assisted the people he loves by making the personal sacrifice of not talking and instead acting out long enough to bring his family to treatment. We'll acknowledge that the torch is officially passed as a way of ending one part of therapy; the no-talk kid can even become our family consultant, depending on circumstances.

From assessment to termination, the therapeutic relationship is different from any other in a child's life. In fact, its success depends in some ways on its ability to end. We achieve our goals, ultimately, by moving from being a real presence to a symbolic one in the child's life, leaving in body but not in significance. If successful, we become an internalized voice reverberating throughout the years with messages of success and connection. But these kids have an enduring effect on us, too. In helping kids terminate well, we are also developing an unusual skill—becoming expert at saying goodbye to children we have learned to love.

10

From Idealism to Burn-out—and Partway Back

THE CHALLENGES OF NO-TALK therapy with children and adolescents exceed those of other treatment approaches. We have fewer techniques to hide behind and more difficult kids to help. We became child therapists because we liked kids and enjoyed being with them. Without being *too* arrogant, we may even have had some faith in our ability to make healing connections that could significantly alter the course of a child's life.

But most child therapists who have been practicing for a while have seen their original hopes and aspirations erode a bit. The kids are more damaged, the environments are more toxic, and, for better or worse, managed care has irrevocably changed the meaning of child treatment. Most child therapists I know talk often about leaving therapy practice for other less taxing work; many already have made this move.

Those of us who are still cleaning Play Doh from the rug at the end of the week need to hold onto our feelings of hope and enthusiasm. But this is not so easy to do. We know that in the course of treating a single kid, we may travel all the way from idealism to burn-out. Even within a therapy hour, we may be aware of feelings as disparate as hope and despair, relaxation and frustration, confidence and fear. This variety of reactions to the kids and the work is actually reassuring; it's when we have only dark feelings that we need to be most concerned.

THE PATH TO BURN-OUT

Idealism

Wanting to help kids has to be one of the most idealistic aspirations around. In graduate school, we build onto the foundation of idealism with compelling theories, fascinating case studies (featuring successful outcomes, orchestrated by charismatic gurus), and, if we're lucky, supportive supervisors. After our coursework and internships are completed, we are as full of idealism—and confidence—as we'll ever be.

We need to protect this idealism, somehow buttressing it against the avalanche of reality that inevitably follows. If we're clever and determined enough, we can tuck it away into a safe corner of our minds. We'll then be able to take it out to feed off it from time to time. Idealism is about helping kids have the childhood that is everyone's birthright to enjoy—free, as James Garbarino (1995) has written, "to play and learn and love, being safe from the pressures of adult economic and sexual forces, and being accepted for who you are and not what you do" (p. 15). It's idealism that gets us out of bed on a dark winter morning, ready to try again. Of course, we must also make room for all the other, more hardened, ways of being that come from experience; we live in the world as it comes to us. But the original hopefulness is vital. While idealism alone can't make connections with kids, it definitely helps.

Curiosity

Idealism leads naturally to emotional and intellectual curiosity. We begin with no-talk kids the way we know how—in the manner we've been taught, seen on videotapes, tried successfully before—and fall flat. These kids are, after all, particularly gifted in behaving unpredictably. In our curious mode we may *wonder*: "Isn't this interesting? My strategies aren't working. I wonder what's different here? I wonder what I could try that might make things progress? I wonder what is going on with this kid?" Our ability to wonder has an enormously productive—and non-defensive—aura about it. Although other, more negative feelings may soon seep in, the longer we can hang onto our curiosity, the more open we remain to change ourselves.

Taken together, idealism and curiosity may sound naive and unprofessional; such childlike qualities seem to reek of inexperience and cluelessness. But, like Picasso, who combined a conscious desire to paint like a child with a sophisticated knowledge of art, we can remain open to wonder without losing our adult perspective. When we stop being curious, we are well on the road to burn-out. It's helpful to be able to see no-talk kids through wondering eyes.

Confusion

After curiosity, confusion inevitably sets in when answers aren't readily at hand. No-talk kids provide scenarios that they didn't tell us about in graduate school. Indeed, books on child therapy give short shrift to no-talk kids, if they're even mentioned at all. We're often led to believe that *we're* the only ones kids aren't talking to—it's our dirty little secret. And we don't really expect this struggle, which makes it even more disorienting.

Confusion can lead us further down burn-out lane if we don't recognize it and remember to keep our heads about us. Like someone who suddenly realizes he is lost in the woods, confused no-talk therapists can either panic or stop and find out where the moss is, or the sun, or the stream. As experts, we're not supposed to be confused, so we tend to stave off this realization for much too long. By then we're likely to be right in the thick of it. But if we acknowledge our bewilderment (to ourselves, at the very least), we can then begin to notice and act on the variables that make this kid and this situation so perplexing.

Frustration

No-talk kids are, by definition, frustrating therapy candidates. They may even take unwarranted pleasure in thwarting us. Even though we may be proficient at helping kids develop greater tolerance for *their* feelings of frustration, we'll have to do some additional work on ours if we want to stay in the action. We need to learn more about our own signs and symptoms of frustration (a tightening of the stomach, sweaty palms, boredom, the onset of irritation) and to monitor these signs throughout our work.

Catching ourselves early on when we begin to get frustrated can keep us thinking clearly and maturely. Once we get too aroused or upset, we'll be problem-solving like a no-talk kid, fueling resentment and anger towards kids, ourselves, past supervisors, Carl Whitaker for making it look so easy, and our neighbor with an easy day job. Once we leave the straightforward situations that keep us confident and intrigued, we need to develop our own set of self-soothing strategies that can help us when we venture into less-comfortable territory.

Irritation

When feelings of frustration go untended in no-talk therapy, they quickly transmute into plain old irritation. This is particularly dangerous for us, because the source of irritation is the symptomatic child we are hoping to help. Most child therapists experience irritation with their young clients more than they admit. Typically, kids who get sent to therapy have a prodigious

repertoire of annoying behaviors, including not talking or playing. The potential for irritation lies in every interaction: Kids
cheat, they make messes they refuse to clean up, they spill
things, they won't come in the office, they won't leave, they
climb on chairs with muddy boots, they pocket little toys that
belong to us, they pretend to go to sleep, they whine and
wheedle about taking our stuff home, and they break brand-new
crayons *on purpose*.

We have to use our sense of humor, curiosity, empathy, and
self-soothing strategies to combat our budding irritation, so it
doesn't fester into something larger and tougher to manage. In
terms of countertransference, irritation is a vivid indication that
we need to examine more closely the "stuff" in us that this child
is pulling up. It's a warning sign that the road ahead is going to
be bumpy indeed unless we quickly do something about our
reaction to this child.

Shame

Being "good with kids" is a big deal for child therapists; this
feeling preserves our dignity and integrity through 27 mind-
numbing games of Candyland. We actually like going into those
multisystemic messes and making sense out of them. Our pride
in our work is fundamental. So when we get nowhere with a no-
talk kid, we soon feel like abject failures and screw-ups. The toll
is heavy indeed. Shame accompanies many of the steps along
the road to burn-out, and it has an insidious effect on our resilience and confidence.

Shame is a primitive feeling, probably dating back to age two
or three; it's the unwanted sensation of being exposed. Since
psychotherapy is a peculiarly private endeavor, the advent of
shame requires special scrutiny. The fact remains that no one
really knows what we do with kids behind the closed doors. And
in traditional therapy we can hide further; behind our professional "blank slate" personas, no one "sees" us. In no-talk therapy,
though, by intent and accident, we are more exposed and less

protected. This vulnerability by itself does not cause us to be ashamed, and it can in fact make us more effective and empathic.

It is when we lose what Erikson (1963) calls "a sense of rightful dignity" (p. 254) toward our work that we become overwhelmed by shame; we feel completely and devastatingly transparent. Suddenly we perceive that people can see how little we really know about child therapy and how meaningless our advanced degrees are. Once we are shaken back to this infantile place, we cannot be effective with kids. When we realize we have become ashamed of our work, we need to make those changes (e.g., supervision, a vacation, our own therapy) that will enable us to regain feelings of competence and autonomy.

Anxiety

Like shame, the river of anxiety may flow beneath the surface of no-talk therapy, sometimes surfacing with a raging current. A little anxiety in the face of working with these kids is okay— provided it lasts for just a few minutes and leads to something more productive. We have to be aware of this worry and fear, and then do something about it. We don't want anxiety that leads to paralysis or anger, but a bit of adrenaline that keeps us alert isn't necessarily a bad thing.

It is also quite possible that the no-talk kid facing us is at least as anxious as we are. This may fuel our own trepidation, and we need to be aware both of our own internal state and what else might happen so that being in the room can feel better for both of us. For example, doing something with our hands (e.g., with markers or clay, or tossing a ball) or listening to music, or playing a fast-paced card game can give things a chance to settle a bit. The main point is to keep tabs on our level of anxiety throughout our work with no-talk kids—and particularly with large and challenging adolescents.

Rage

Although burn-out is a more serious condition, rage is probably the ugliest and most countertherapeutic emotional state. A kid alone can occasionally get the bile going—being so provocative, cruel, or harmful that we lose our grip on ourselves, but this occurs only rarely. More often, a series of events will conspire to undermine us, penetrating our defenses so we can barely do our jobs.

Some examples: foster kids are forced to have unsupervised visits with frightening parents, reunification plans drag on long past the "shelf life" of the involved children, teachers keep agitated kids in from recess as a form of discipline, oppositional teens are dropped from social-skills groups (which are designed for kids with social problems), bright kids doing "C" work are denied services, parents bring kids in erratically, funding for just the right program dries up—and the list goes on. If several factors in the environment undo many weeks of our work, we're apt to feel like blowing a gasket.

Under these circumstances, therapy can be a Sisyphean labor, and it's easy to summon pure rage at the systems around a child for continuing to harm him this way. But until the treatment plan changes, kids will often have to hang on in that classroom, undergo visits with those parents, miss us, and experience failure over and over again. We have to be careful that we are following the child's emotional agenda and not presuming to set it for her. It is likely that these kids have a much more complicated, and more distressing, set of feelings than just anger. Thus, while our rage may be justifiable, it has little place in the therapy room.

Panic

Panic is what happens when we say "Beam me up, Scotty," and we find ourselves still in our offices, with 48 minutes to go. Presumably, experienced therapists don't often get this far along in distress before seeking supervision, taking a vacation, attending a conference, or doing *something* to regain personal balance. But panicky feelings can and do arise from time to time with particularly defiant no-talk kids. In these cases, it may be necessary to employ a whole range of self-soothing, problem-solving, and recharging strategies before resuming active therapy. At the least, panic tells us that our personal and professional plans for the day—or week, month, or year—need to be revamped entirely.

Hopelessness and Despair

It's a fact: We can't help some kids. Despair can mean two things: the hard truth or burn-out—or both. Sometimes it is tough to tell the difference anyway. Though this may seem a matter of semantics, it's not. In truth-despair a therapist concludes that this particular kid, in his special circumstances, with his unique history, cannot be reached at this time, in this way, by this therapist. It is a very specific kind of hopelessness and may even contain the belief that at another time, with someone else, there could be hope. Sometimes kids need to go through five or six therapists before they're ready to work. In truth-despair, we view this situation as part of our lot in life—it's heartbreaking but we have our limits.

In despair arising from burn-out, however, we throw up our hands and say things like "The world is going to hell in a handbasket," "I think I should go into advertising," and "These kids are driving me crazy." We move rapidly from the specific impasse to the general hopelessness. This is a serious condition signaling that we are no longer effective therapists.

BURN-OUT AND COMPASSION FATIGUE

Burning out from treating disturbed and traumatized kids is a serious and real problem. Most of the research to date on therapist burn-out focuses primarily on the impact of hearing too many adult trauma stories. But it's not much of a leap to suggest that the pain of working with victimized kids is just as intense. The few accounts that exist of therapists' personal reactions to their child clients amply support this supposition (e.g., Dyregrov & Mitchell, 1992; James, 1994; Lyon, 1993; Pearce & Pezzot-Pearce, 1997).

The problems of therapist burn-out are so prevalent that researchers have provided a variety of terms to describe the same basic experience: secondary traumatic stress disorder, covictimization, contact victimization, traumatic countertransference, emotional contagion, burn-out, secondary victimization, secondary catastrophic stress reaction, vicarious traumatization, the messiah trap, and (perhaps the most descriptive) compassion fatigue (e.g., Berry, 1989; Dyregrov & Mitchell, 1992; Figley, 1995; Grosch & Olsen, 1994; Herman, 1992).

Symptoms of compassion fatigue are identical to PTSD. However, in this case the cause is exposure to a child's trauma: We become overwhelmed by knowledge of events that have not necessarily happened to us directly. By the time we reach this point, we are having doubts that touch our core beliefs about who we are, what kind of world we live in, and even our spirituality—the very meaning of our lives. We feel the impact of the trauma on our lives in one or more of five critical areas: safety, trust, esteem, intimacy, and control. A disruption in any one or more of these can destroy our ability to function personally and professionally. Compassion fatigue compromises important abilities that we need to be therapists: maintaining a relatively positive sense of self, modulating strong affect, and sustaining an inner sense of connection with others.

Compassion fatigue typically results from an onslaught of factors that undermine our need to feel strong and balanced. These may include being surrounded by traumatic stories, being empathic to the people we treat, having unresolved trauma in our own lives, and making profound connections between the trauma of clients and our own. This last factor appears to be especially true when we deal with the trauma of children (e.g., Dyregrov & Mitchell, 1992; Pearce & Pezzot-Pearce, 1997).

Personal Impact

Compassion fatigue can have a broad-ranging personal impact on us and affect our cognitive, emotional, behavioral, spiritual, interpersonal, and physical functioning. As with victims of primary PTSD, we may become more vulnerable by day or night, alone or with others. The effects of this work can be sudden— upon hearing the details of a particularly horrendous life story— or gradual, over time, through the accumulation of pain that finally breaks down our carefully constructed professional walls. Either way, we are left more fragile and take home with us only the burden of the work, without the pleasure.

Professional Impact

Of course, burn-out has a distinct professional impact as well. With compassion fatigue, we may feel we have to be on auto-pilot just to get through the day. Our morale suffers dramatically, and we're despondent, morose, deflated by the hopelessness of it all. We may begin avoiding our colleagues, hiding out in our offices, retreating from the usual supports we once enjoyed. We may stop making the necessary collateral calls to schools, social service agencies, foster parents, and managed-care plans that are part of our kid work. Others may even notice that we are acting differently before we realize it ourselves. We go to work because we must, without any of the love and idealism we once embodied.

Special Challenges for No-Talk Therapy

No-talk therapists may be more vulnerable to compassion fatigue because empathy is such a centerpiece of our work. By definition, this primary treatment tool is subject to wear and tear. But other aspects of this work also make us more susceptible.

Boundaries

The violation of personal boundaries is at the core of abuse. With all trauma survivors, in all modes of therapy, we have to be aware of and maintain these boundaries with complete integrity. With kids, however, keeping physically separate isn't always possible or advisable. No-talk therapists walk the thinnest line here, since we do not, in every circumstance, abhor touch. It is probably true that the safer the boundaries are, the less likely that we will burn out. But if there is too great a distance, we will not be able to reach no-talk kids.

The boundaries are also theoretical; we need to be clear about the nature of the helping relationship and the therapy itself. This is tricky because the therapeutic relationship is a primary "technique" of our work; it's hard to use it sparingly. We have to establish sensible personal boundaries, to be careful about what we disclose about our "real lives," how much we share, under what kinds of conditions, and how we describe ourselves and our own families. We need to be thoughtfully aware of how much we can meld our personal and professional selves. We've got to be practical, too. We're less likely to burn out if we know the bounds of our ability to help kids. However humbling it may be, knowing our limits may be the best way to prevent compassion fatigue.

Countertransference

At some point in treatment with traumatized no-talk kids, when we are not taking sufficient care of ourselves, we may find our own agendas subsuming the child's needs. We may become overprotective, perhaps delaying the progress of treatment by not wanting to rush the vulnerable child to tell or play out his story. Here we may join the conspiracy of silence, keeping the child in the no-talk mode because we suspect the story is too painful to hear. We may not want to upset a child who appears fragile. We may not want to hear the viciousness of his revenge fantasies (or to consider our own). Because these child stories can provoke our own trauma, because we want so much to keep therapy safe and neutral, because we are empathic, we set the stage for prolonging the no-talk mode long after it is indicated or therapeutically advisable.

If we *overidentify* with a child or adolescent's pain, we'll be unprepared to address upsetting issues or to cope with intense emotions. Our own anxiety and impending burn-out lead to pacing treatment based on our own internal state. We stop responding to the child's need for permission to tell her story and to feel her own feelings.

The Lone Ranger Shrink Rides Again

Even though we try to ensure the presence of a stable circle of adults around a child, almost all kid therapists harbor child-saving fantasies. These may even extend to a desire to scoop a kid into our arms and take him home. Part of the Lone Ranger Shrink syndrome is never saying "no" to a kid who needs us. Though it's one of the most frequent causes of burn-out, the Lone Ranger Shrink makes herself available to the child and family any time of the day or night.

The desire to rescue kids can be overwhelming. In L.R.S. mode, we tend to forget that we're not being as helpful as we imagine for a kid who needs more than one person can give him. It is extremely rare that the personal sacrifice is worth it over the long haul. As the old Hopi saying warns, "one finger cannot pick up a pebble."

Money and Time: Other Stresses

No-talk therapy includes a lot of stresses, even when we do all we can to take care of ourselves. Money is often a problem, and we *never*, *ever* get paid for all of the time we put into a case. It's a fact of the work that can take on quite ugly dimensions if other rewards are also slow in coming. Kid cases are often billing disasters. A noncustodial parent may be responsible for the bill and refuse to pay it, collateral time is usually not reimbursed, kids may come without adults to sessions so no one makes copayments and, on occasion, even with sincere effort, it's just plain hard to find someone to hold financially accountable. And with the advent of managed care, we must also spend considerable, nonreimbursed time repeating case histories and treatment plans every several weeks in order to schedule necessary sessions.

As anyone who has been on teams can attest, we can also spend inordinate amounts of time getting everyone up to speed and working collaboratively. The circle of adults seldom includes participants of equal competence. In no-talk therapy, the "team" can be amorphous and contain players of wide-ranging ability, interest, participation, and empathy. When time is so precious, it can be utterly demoralizing to spend it with people who have more power than insight. But if team meetings become the-therapist-versus-the-system or the-therapist-runs-the-show, burn-out may be just around the corner. Finally, it must be noted that no-talk kids invariably come from depleted family and community systems that may well be struggling with compassion fatigue of their own. By the time a no-talk kid is in therapy, he'll have left many exhausted adults in his wake.

SURVIVAL AND PREVENTION STRATEGIES

Compassion fatigue is not an inevitability of no-talk therapy. But we *do* need to develop personal, professional and environmental stratgies for managing these tough cases. Successful survival tactics don't necessarily require daily meditation or annual vacations in Bermuda, though these activities can help. The most important consideration is pacing; we should give a variety of strategies regular attention over time.

Personal Strategies

It's not "just a job," but we do need to have real lives of our own outside the office. This seems almost too obvious to state, but far too many child therapists don't make the time to play when they're not at work. Some of our non-work time needs to be relaxing—being out in nature, doing art or music, hobbies, yoga, learning new skills that have nothing to do with therapy. Any avocation that is both fun and restorative counts. Therapists with families at home tend to give all the time, everywhere. Thus, engaging in activities that don't involve caring for anyone else can provide a vital break from work.

We've got to develop a network of emotionally supportive relationships outside of the office. Again, this might be one of these "No, duh," kinds of observations, but anecdotal evidence suggests that many therapists rely heavily upon their work setting for their social lives. We need to have people around us who are thinking about other things besides therapy. We need friends who will listen and help *us*. Once we stop *getting* support, our capacity to provide it is sadly diminished.

We want to maintain an early warning system for our own emotional state. Taking time for self-exploration, our own therapy, spiritual practice, diversion, and replenishment makes us better and more balanced therapists. Once we lose our perspective—and our sense of humor—we're just rearranging deck chairs on the Titanic.

Finally, attending to our physical health can benefit our work with no-talk kids. At the very least, we've got to sustain a high level of energy to play and engage with children. Thus, we should take seriously the lifestyle that is now proven to make a difference: exercise, good food, sleep, down-time, daylight, vacations, and staying away from chemicals. Therapists frequently ask clients about these natural anti-stress and anti-depression

strategies while sucking down their fifth cup of coffee after a
late night. We have to take care of ourselves in order to take
care of kids.

Professional Strategies

Burn-out prevention also requires that we take a close look at
how we engage in professional practice. While therapists working exclusively with adults can manage an isolated solo work
life, this is poor advice for doing therapy with kids. We need to
have adults around for peer supervision and consultation—and
just to keep our sanity. A few intelligent and witty grown-ups
nearby can keep us energized and provide a needed balance to a
day that is otherwise spent crosslegged on the floor making car
noises. Good colleagues check out kids in the waiting room,
consult in the halls, provide back-up, and taste burnt cookies.
They provide ongoing informal consultation—often more valuable than hours of paid supervision. For example, we may ask a
colleague to sit in the waiting room and observe or speak to the
seven-year-old who is hiding under the couch there. After our
session, we can discuss the child informed by our experience and
our colleague's observations and hunches.

If it's at all possible, it helps to diversify our practices. A few
no-talk kids are plenty, particularly if they are also traumatized
and furious. It's rejuvenating to see a range of kids and families
and to have the satisfaction of people getting better quickly with
a strategic intervention or two. Treating enuresis or a simple
phobia or designing an effective behavioral program can work
wonders for us as well. Similarly, it's a pleasure to see a few
adults who do all the things in therapy we think they should—
talk, reflect, practice, interact, tell their friends about us. Variety
is not only the spice of life but also a great buffer to compassion
fatigue.

Providing and receiving continuing education also keep us on
our theoretical toes in vital ways. Not only does the time out
from clinical work help on its own, but training and exchange

with other therapists are essential if our work is to remain fresh and interesting. Like tennis lessons, continuing education keeps us from practicing our bad habits and gives us a few new ideas to try out. The informal exchanges that take place at conferences, during question-and-answer sessions, and in hotel lobbies, can lead us to some creative interventions for our particularly sticky cases. Child therapy is more of an art than a science. We learn formally, through lectures and texts, and informally, from other child therapists describing solutions of their own.

Maintaining a balanced outlook toward our work is another important aspect of professional survival. We need to sustain clear professional boundaries, setting limits on what we expect of ourselves—and permit others to expect from us. It helps to seek out support and guidance in a systematic way, not just when we are drowning. This means we benefit most from finding colleagues, supervisors, and managers we can trust and respect.

We have to heed the warning signs when our enthusiasm, curiosity, and idealism are on the wane. Are we clock-watching, counting down the hours until we can go home, playing a game that requires as little of our attention as possible, writing a letter while on the phone, or somehow detatching from the therapy and the child? It's important to plan ahead and decide how we will cope when this happens. If we begin to despair, we need to employ strategies that return us to a healthier, replenished feeling about our work. In addition, we must periodically reevaluate our jobs and the nature of our commitment to them. In this era of managed care, most of our work is more task-oriented than it once was. We need to assess honestly what we must do to maintain our sense of professional integrity and then act accordingly.

Environmental Strategies

The cloistered sanctuary of the therapist's office is a charming notion of a bygone era. It's no longer possible to practice in some kind of value-free (and socially irresponsible) manner. We have to attend to the social policies that have created this generation of increasingly troubled kids and provided so few supports to aid them. If we persist in addressing problems of the culture and community as individual deviance, we will surely burn out— and be less effective.

Kids need advocates even more than they need therapists. For kids, such advocacy can mean going to school meetings, writing letters of recommendation, or showing up at the band performance even when family members are unable or unwilling to attend. Within the family, advocacy occurs when parents are given the support and skills necessary to protect their children and adolescents, when families help these kids make constructive and empathic decisions, when trauma symptoms have a safe place to resolve.

In the community, advocacy can include sitting on the board of the local Y or teen center, public speaking on topics of child and adolescent development, and helping to develop needed community resources and programs. Advocacy through social policy is knowing who the policy makers are, finding out about the issues they are concerned with, and lobbying them through the mail, on the phone, and in person. As an antidote to compassion fatigue, a little social action goes a long way. It broadens our personal and professional identity, it includes the child's context in the activity we call therapy, and it holds the potential for making our jobs easier some day in the future.

The rewards of successful no-talk therapy are well worth the attention we give to burn-out prevention. The strategies that work can be summarized by three directives: First, *take stock*. Lead an examined, adult life. Make sure that being a kid therapist is a good idea. Second, *take a stand*. Speak up for kids, for what is really important. Care. Third, *take a vacation*. Don't make this work all there is to life. Fish, dance, sing, get a dog, meditate, bake bread. The idealism we once felt about our work doesn't have to disappear amid all our experience.

There's much we can do to keep hopeful feelings alive in our work, hold compassion fatigue at bay *and* make a difference in the life of a child. As we foster the resilience of no-talk kids, we give them the skills and resources they desperately need. With connection and success in different areas of their lives, children can develop voices that ring strong and true.

Appendix

Gimmicks, Gadgets,
and Games

THIS APPENDIX PROVIDES an alphabetical compendium of activities that work in no-talk therapy. While this reference section could never be complete, it offers a multitude of methods to help get unstuck in a session and can serve as a springboard for new ideas. Most child therapists have a few tricks of their own; each no-talk kid offers the opportunity to figure out some more.

Affirmations

No-talk kids have a steady stream of negative thoughts they may say about themselves. With failure so much a part of their lives, they are too familiar with those toxic voices. The affirmation, then, becomes a possible first step in counteracting some of the destructive self-talk that readily becomes self-fulfilling prophecy. What Beverly James (1989) has called "Booster messages" can be put on T-shirts and banners, imprinted on pencils, ordered on return-address labels, and turned into song. If kids aren't ready to practice saying things like, "I am a loveable child," "I deserve to be happy," "I have a right to all of my feelings," "I can control my temper. . . ." or any other hopeful or positive statement, we can mail affirmations to them in a letter. "It was great seeing you yesterday. I admire your courage. You can be afraid and you can act anyway. . . . " We can put a boxful of affirmations in front of them and have them select one at random. We can give them a book or a calendar of affirmations to refer to each day. Or we can pick out a favorite affirmation and together make a poster out of it, decorated and illustrated, for the no-talk kid to take home and put on her wall. There are numerous books of affirmations for children and adolescents on the market. These include, for example:

- Wardon, M. (1993). *101 affirmations for teenagers.* Group Publishing.
- Bowen, C. (1995). *I believe in me.* Unity Press.
- Payne, L. (1994). *Just because I am: A child's book of affirmations.* Free Spirit Publishing.
- Bloch, D., & Merritt, J. (1993). *Positive self-talk for children: Teaching self-esteem through affirmations: A guide for parents, teachers and counselors.* Bantam.

Applause Box

The Applause Box is a gag gift that may be found in some novelty shops. Shapiro (1994) has invented a personalized version that carries even more therapeutic clout. With a tape recorder and a tape, assemble family (or the special education team!) and enough other people to make a lot of noise. At least five people are needed. Signal the group to applaud all at once, the louder the better. After about 10 seconds of enthusiastic applause, ask three or four people to make specific comments directly into the microphone, with the applause continuing in the background. For example, have Mom say, "I'm so proud of you," or a brother say, "Way to go, you did it," or Dad say, "Wonderful job, we love you." When a no-talk kid makes a step in the right direction, a little applause can be a real reward for good work in therapy, and a gift when the treatment is done.

Art

As a nonverbal form of communication, few activities are better suited to no-talk therapy than art projects. These can be paintings, sculptures, drawings, or collages, using pens, pencils, markers, tempera paints, watercolors, fingerpaints, clay, Play Doh, or some other media. Kids can make art spontaneously, picking up materials that just happen to be lying around. Some adolescents are more able to talk and focus when their hands are busy making art.

Therapists can also structure requests for a painting or drawing for assessment purposes (asking the child to draw a specific item) or for catharsis (asking the child to draw how she feels). Both the process of creating art and the product are the stuff of no-talk treatment; kids may want to take work home or have it displayed in the office. A particularly informative art project is the family crest/family shield; the child (and even the family) designs and develops a shield with symbols of three or four things about them on the front.

Collaborative art projects are fun and include, for example, mutual "story telling," in which therapist and child take turns drawing events in an unfolding tale, and the Squiggle Game (Winnicott, 1971), in which therapist and child take turns making a squiggle and then turning it into a picture of something. Some no-talk kids enjoy having their own roll of paper, adding to it with a new drawing each week. The roll then becomes a kind of "case history" of the treatment. With collaborative art, no one is in charge and no one does it "the right way," which can be extremely freeing for kids who feel powerless much of the time.

Astrology

Even those among us who think astrology is a tad hokey may admit to feeling a certain amusement with what our signs and the stars have to tell us. In any case, some kids are quite committed to their horoscopes. The process of learning about how to "do" astrology has some excellent no-talk kid properties: It can take a long time to learn how to draw charts, the subject readily lures no-talk kids into a contemplation of the characteristics they share with their "sign," and astrology can generate speculations about relationships. Kids can wonder about what aspects of their personality (or sign) clash or meld with other personalities. A few helpful titles on the prodigious astrology bookshelf include:

- George, D. (1988). *Astrology for yourself: How to understand and interpret your own birth chart: A workbook for personal transformation.* Wingbow.
- Marks, T. (1986). *The art of chart interpretation.* CRCS Publications.
- Parker, J. (1995). *The astrologer's handbook.* CRCS Publications.
- Sakoian, F., & Acker, L. (1989). *The astrologer's handbook.* HarperCollins.
- Arroyo, S. & Marshall, J. (1990). *Chart interpretation handbook.* CRCS Publications.
- Oken, A. (1989). *Alan Oken's complete astrology.* Bantam Doubleday Dell.
- Woolfolk, J. (1990). *The only astrology book you'll ever need.* Scarborough House.

Athletics

In addition to connecting kids to opportunities to participate in real sports with other kids, no-talk therapy by itself can raise a sweat. In the office, a variety of Nerf balls can encourage "dialogue" through a game of catch or a free-throw shooting match with a basketball hoop. Most toy stores now have safe, indoor nerf-type darts, bowling sets, boomerangs, frisbees, golf clubs, and bats. On a more contained note, a table can be converted for tabletop football or hockey, or small-sized ping-pong.

A trip to the park can also provide athletic "treatment"—

watching a no-talk kid perform stunts on a skateboard, having a game of catch or hacky-sack, jumping rope, or juggling, for example. For kids who need to stay active to feel in control, therapy focused on athletics may be the only viable course of treatment.

Bibliotherapy

Using books as part of a kid's treatment can take many forms, all of which can provide both information and connection in the therapy.

Topical Books

These are books that address specific problems (e.g., divorce, eating disorders, stepfamilies, abuse, compulsions, attention and learning problems, hospitalization, anger, new siblings) written for kids and teenagers. Such books can be read in therapy, given as gifts, or assigned as homework. Not only are they educational, but they also help break the isolation that these kids commonly experience. Three good places to find topical books for kids are in annotated bibliographies on children's literature, the Childswork Childsplay catalogue (800-962-1141), or on the World Wide Web at amazon.com.

Storybooks

Illustrated children's books are also staples of no-talk therapy, especially for younger kids (although many early adolescents may also enjoy the comforting regressive pull of a good picture book). Storybooks can be used for a quiet, comforting cuddle on the couch with a small child (e.g., *Goodnight Moon*) or as a vehicle to get a useful message across (e.g., *The Little Engine that Could*). There are also illustrated books about death, foster care, abuse, and almost every other imaginable problem. It's impossible to devise an ideal list, and time spent browsing in a bookstore with a good children's section will seldom be wasted. Some enduring titles include:

- Aliki (1984). *Feelings*. Mulberry.
- Asch, F. (1986) *Goodbye house*. Prentice-Hall.
- Berenstain, S., & J. *Berenstain Bears* (series). First Time.
- Brown, M. (1947). *Goodnight moon*. Harper.
- Piper, W. (1930). *The little engine that could*. Platt & Munk.
- Gag, W. (1928). *Millions of cats*. Coward.
- Gerstein, M. (1987). *The mountains of Tibet*. Harper.
- Kraus, R. (1987). *Leo the late bloomer*. Harpercollins.
- Leaf, M. (1936). *The story of Ferdinand*. Puffin.
- Mayer, M. *Little Monster* (series). Cartwheel.
- Miles, M. (1971). *Annie and the old one*. Little, Brown.
- Rogers, F. *Mr. Rogers* (series). Putnam.
- Ray, H (1941). *Curious George*. Houghton.
- Slobodkina, E. (1947). *Caps for sale*. Harper.
- Steig, W. (1986). *Brave Irene*. Farrar Straus.
- Thompson, K. (1955). *Eloise*. Simon & Schuster.
- Viorst, J. (1972). *Alexander and the terrible, horrible, no good, very bad day*. Aladdin.
- Williams. M. (1922). *The velveteen rabbit*. Avon.
- Winthrop, E. (1985). *Tough Eddie*. Dutton.
- Zolotow, C. (1972). *William's doll*. Harper.

Co-authored Books
Either written longhand or on the computer, a shared story can be a splendid no-talk task. We might also illustrate the tale together and make a suitable cover. The book can be purely silly, a fantasy story, a revision of a classic fairy tale, or a guide for other kids who have a similar problem. The process here is usually more important than either the content or the product; indeed, this may be the first occasion in a child's life when she has co-authored anything.

Workbooks

These highly structured and solution-focused books can be used
in the office, with parents, or by the older child on his own.
Workbooks have been developed for a range of problems and
include, for example (from Childswork Childsplay unless otherwise noted):

- *The self-control patrol workbook*
- *The cooperation workbook*
- *Jumpin' Jake settles down: A workbook to help impulsive children learn
  to think before they act*
- *How I learned to make friends: A storybook and workbook of activities
  to help children make friends*
- *Angry monster workbook*
- *The problem-solving workbook*
- *The coping skills workbook*
- *The kids' solutions workbook*
- *The teens' solutions workbook*
- *The divorce workbook: A guide for kids and families* (Waterfront
  Books, 1985)

As this incomplete list may suggest, workbooks are a growing
part of bibliotherapy. In the early stages, of course, no-talk treatment steers away from excessive focus on problems. But down
the road workbooks can provide a nice transition between no-
talk and talk if problems persist despite the newfound competencies.

Bubbles and Bubble Pipes

Kids of all ages like blowing bubbles. This activity is inexpen-
sive, relaxing, and enjoyable. Bubble pipes have an added benefit; they can be used in conjunction with teaching relaxation
skills. Making bubbles come out of a pipe develops focusing and
deep breathing. Watching bubbles float and pop can be used for
relationship-building, self-soothing, and problem-solving (I won-

der which bubble will pop first, float highest, grow biggest. . .). Most important, it is hard to be angry or anxious while blowing bubbles.

Building

Construction activities cross gender and age and are among the most satisfying no-talk projects. Toy stores and hardware stores are filled with kits for assembling things. For those near woods or parks, the outdoors also provides interesting construction materials. Books on crafts and projects for kids abound; a few of the many titles include:

- Hamilton, L. (1991). *Child's play 6–12*. Crown.
- Lehne, J. (1992). *Never be bored book*. Sterling.
- Einon, D. (1985). *Play with a purpose*. Pantheon.

Building fulfills many different goals of treatment: It involves planning, following directions, sharing materials, relatively rapid (but not immediate) accomplishment, turn-taking, and a product to be proud of. These kinds of projects can take a few minutes, an entire session, or weeks and weeks, depending upon the developmental level and interest of the no-talk kid. Some building ideas include:

- bird houses
- model cars, boats, and planes (snap together and glue)
- popsicle-stick boxes and houses
- dream catchers
- tin-punch lanterns
- mobiles
- cardboard tube rockets
- cardboard box pet houses, or doll houses, or forts
- pine cone, soda bottle, and milk carton bird feeders

Another kind of construction project is building a "community" out of found materials. Outside, rocks, leaves, twigs, acorns, and grass can be used to make a miniature neighborhood. Indoors, cereal boxes, tape, candy wrappers, Popsicle sticks, and cardboard may be used. Kids can use recycled junk to create an entire world of their own.

Cat's Cradle/String Games

String games provide the opportunity for a nonverbal dialogue, passing a transforming loop back and forth, learning complex designs, and sharing in a nonstressful activity. There are more than 40 string games around. See, for example:

- Gryski, C. (1983). *String games*. Kids Can Press.
- Foerder, M. (1996). *String games*. Golden Books.

Clay

Clay, in its many varied forms, is a satisfyingly messy and regressive activity that can engage even the most cynical and disengaged no-talk kid. Some varieties of "clay" include: flour dough, salt dough, cornstarch clay, Glarch—made from Elmer's glue and liquid starch (all of which are homemade), plaster, Play Doh, Sculpy, plasticine, and regular drying clay. Kids can do any number of therapeutic activities with clay, including:

- fooling around
- making a sculpture
- making and throwing "clay bombs" at a drawn outline of an offending person, accompanied by angry comments. Beverly James (1989) first described this use of a bucket of clay as a way to help kids restructure traumatizing events. Wads of wet paper towels also work well. So do eggs heaved at trees

in the woods. For a more detailed description of this activity, see James (1989.)

- making symbolic, non-human models of various family members
- making characters that are part of a larger project (e.g., soldiers for a fort, a family for a doll house, animals for an ark or zoo, etc.)

Clowning

Kids know that clowns are free to act in outrageous ways, even if they don't say a word. While some teenagers may be too inhibited to don a little face paint and a red nose, this activity can be liberating for many kids, as they decide who their clown "persona" is. This alter ego can be bossy, mean, shy, silly, powerful, tricky, or sad. No matter what they choose they are sharing a part of themselves.

Computers

Computers, and the side-by-side stance they require, can take a central place in no-talk therapy. Computers offer a way to display competencies, reveal frustration tolerance, and increase therapy compliance. Some of their many uses include:

- watching a game of skill played by a no-talk kid
- taking turns playing a computer game
- taking turns writing a computer story
- looking up something serious or frivolous on the World Wide Web
- e-mail
- getting help on how to use a program (many kids are more computer-literate than we are)

Construction Supplies

A good variety of construction supplies on hand ensures the rapid enagagement of younger kids, and some diversion for the fidgety no-talk adolescent. These may include, for example, Legos, Lincoln Logs, Tinkertoys, K'nex, Erector Sets, and good old wooden blocks.

Cooking

Depending on the kitchen facilities in an office, "cooking" projects can be as simple as heating a can of soup or some instant pudding or as complex as making cookies from scratch. Many children's cooking and activity books have good ideas. See for example:

- Magee, E. (1997). *Someone's in the kitchen with mommy.* NCT Contemporary Publishing.
- Everyday Chef (1998) *Cooking with kids.*
- Edge, N. (1979). *Kids in the kitchen.* Peninsula.

Here are a few projects that don't require a cookbook to complete:

- soup and crackers
- microwave snacks
- "ants on a log" (peanut butter and raisins on celery sticks)
- "instant" snacks (e.g., juice from powder, pudding from a mix)
- blender shakes

Projects that lead to eating are usually very successful. However, in addition to the range of recipes for consumption by humans, other "cooking" projects can lead to bird food (e.g., pine cone feeders), dyes and inks (e.g., made with berries, kitchen spices, coffee grounds, and vegetables), stamping messages (carved into raw potatoes or apples), and potpourri (from outdoors, spice racks, and craft shops).

Costumes

A box with interesting fabrics, boas, wigs, props, and hats in it can delight kids of a wide range of ages. And posing as someone else altogether, kids may be more likely to speak!

Some no-talk kids may also be interested in making a personal "power cape," with designs on it symbolizing the hidden superpowers they posess when they wear it.

Diplomas and Certificates

In no-talk therapy, we are ever on the lookout for positive change, and quick to acknowledge it. One method of recognition elevates the achievement to a ceremony. Diplomas and certificates are powerful reinforcers for kids, simultaneously symbolizing what has been accomplished and increasing the likelihood that gains will be maintained.

David Epston and his narrative therapy colleagues are endlessly inventive about finding occasions to honor a child in a ceremony. They draw up "letters of reference" for membership in "clubs" (e.g., The Temper Tamer's Club, The Fear Facers, The Worry Stoppers Club, The Peace Family Project, The Freedom from 'Ferpection' Network; Freeman, Epston, & Lobovits, 1997). These awards shift therapy from a primary focus on individual and family change toward a broader cultural perspective on problems.

Even without membership in a larger society, kids can receive awards for all manner of milestones: school attendance, controlling their tempers, negotiating with parents, staying in the therapy room for the hour, even watering plants. Diplomas can be created on the computer, or in longhand, and bestowed with varying degrees of ceremony and audience participation, depending upon the event.

Face Painting/Facials

Face painting for younger kids and facials for older girls both get kids looking in the mirror and touching their faces as they make different expressions. This can be valuable both for the self-care involved and emotions aroused.

Feelings

The language of feelings develops over time, but it helps to have a good feeling vocabulary on hand. Some useful words include: surprised, hurt, silly, smart, irritable, upset, worried, interested, proud, loving, sad, unsure, excited, scared, confused, anxious, sorry, bored, satisfied, thoughtful, lonely, angry, cranky, dreamy, affectionate, happy, nervous, stressed, concerned, devastated, pleased, guilty, stunned, fed up, attentive, peaceful, embarrassed, disappointed, greedy, shy, brave, jealous, shocked, sick, tired. . . Using such words, there are many beneficial feeling exercises and activities:

Picture Dictionaries
Have the no-talk kid write a feeling on the top of a piece of paper and look through magazines and photographs to find someone with that expression on his face. Take turns drawing people or animals expressing these feelings. Cut out and glue the picture below the feeling word.

Mirrors
Many no-talk kids do not know what feelings look like, and they misread other people's expressions. With a mirror they can watch themselves make faces and interpret the way their emotional state appears to others.

Charades
Put feeling words in a bowl and take turns picking and acting out the word for the other to guess.

Baskets

This technique, developed by Beverly James (1989), helps kids recognize and express contradictory feelings. The basket can contain pens, poker chips, even paper clips—as long as it has lots of that particular item. The participants take turns thinking up feelings and writing them in big letters, each on its own piece of paper laid on the table. For example, they might write three feelings: mad, sad, and worried. Then, holding the basket of "feelings chips," they take turns considering a recent event that aroused some feelings. For example, the child may recall that the teacher made fun of him in school and assign the most "feelings chips" to the *mad* paper, some to the *sad* paper, and a few to the *worried* paper. The therapist then takes the basket and describes an event in her life that produced mixed feelings, assigning her chips accordingly.

Aquariums

Fill an aquarium with rocks, each with a feeling word written on it. Have the child fish out a rock each week and tell something that happened to him associated with this feeling.

Colors

Kids are asked to make a list of feelings along one side of a piece of paper; we can help them if they seem stumped. Each feeling is written in a specific color selected by the child, so that the list becomes its own kind of color key. Then the child proportionally fills in a big circle with the colors to describe how she is feeling or has felt at particular times. Beverly James (1989) also uses these color keys to have the child make a color timeline, beginning at birth and continuing up to the present. Kids represent in colors how they have felt at different times during their lives. It can also be useful to have them continue the color timeline into the future. No-talk kids need to wonder who they are becoming, and what they will do and feel in the years to come.

Folded Paper

Have the child draw a picture on the outside of a piece of folded paper that represents how everyone sees him. Then have him open the paper and, on the inside, draw a picture of how he really feels.

Board Games

There are several fine games on the market that are played to elicit feelings from kids (e.g., "The Talking, Feeling and Doing Game," "The Ungame," "The Great Feelings Chase"—all available from Childswork Childsplay). For a comprehensive review of the most popular therapy games, see Shapiro (1993).

It can also be fun to invent a board game from scratch. This can be played very simply (e.g., make a spinner with feeling words on it. Then, earn chips by taking turns spinning and describing a time when the feeling was dominant). Inventing games can also be a more complicated endeavor, taking several sessions to complete; designing the board, figuring out the rules, and making the cards are all interesting and productive activities. Existing checker, chess, and other game boards can be transformed, or the entire product can be made from scratch. Game-making kits are available in toystores, and through Creative Education of Canada (800-982-2642).

Boats

Therapists practicing near a stream or river might help kids make little boats out of found materials and put in the boat a picture or message of a fear or a wish to send out symbolically to the sea. (These messages or pictures can also be sent to the sky in a helium balloon.)

Fortune Tellers

Fortune tellers appeal to the magical sensibilities of kids. With the Magic-Eight Ball or a crystal ball, kids share their concerns and hopes for the future through the various fortune-telling activities. A fine way to get started is:

- Klutz Press (1998). *The cootie-catcher book: Tear 'em out, fold 'em up fortune tellers.* Klutz Press.

Games

When in doubt, play a game. The standard office supply might include a few of the following (because therapists should not keep games they loathe, noisy games like Operation are omitted from this list):

- Parcheesi
- Monopoly
- Connect Four
- Uno
- Life
- Cards and poker chips
- Twister
- Guess Who
- Trouble
- Chinese Checkers
- Dominoes
- Lotto
- Pick-up Sticks
- Chutes and Ladders
- Othello
- Yahtzee
- Sorry
- Checkers
- Chess
- Pictionary
- Clue
- Scrabble
- Boggle
- Jacks

Garbage Bags

This activity, adapted from James (1989), is useful when some therapeutic relationship is already developed and we have a sense of a history of shame and secrecy that has led to the unwillingness to talk. Traumatic events, upsetting interactions, and problems of all kinds can be described in writing and then placed in a garbage bag. The bag, decorated as the child desires, symbolizes the way people carry around difficult experiences and become burdened with them, as though they were smelly garbage. And, as James notes, "The overpowering incidents that the child has experienced are literally contained (in a bag in the therapist's office), and because the events have become concretized, the child gains a much needed sense of control" (p. 167). Variations on garbage bags include a box of burdens and a worry box.

Going Places

If sitting in the therapy room is not going anywhere, it is time to go outside. Depending upon the child's home situation, parents can be helped as well by accompanying the traveling treatment to the library, a pet store, a museum, the park, an ice cream shop, a hospital, a record store, a hobby shop, the zoo, an art supply store, a bookstore, or some other destination of mutual interest. Take kids to places that guarantee success—a library or toy store—and where they'll be treated respectfully.

Watching animals interact can be particularly fascinating as a prelude to conversation. Sometimes just a quiet walk around the block or to the corner store for a soda begins to build a connection. It can also be a valuable no-talk experience to follow the child's directions for where to turn or stop—kids are often delighted to control what happens in the hour.

Travel can also have deeper meaning. For example, a trip to a bridge can be used to symbolize the connection between two sets of experiences. Similarly, kids can take therapists to places that are significant to them, e.g., old houses, schools, playgrounds, the hospital emergency room, or a previous foster home.

Growing Plants

Depending upon available space and light, some leafy plants, flowers, and vegetables are quite hardy and easy to grow indoors. Growing plants has few rivals as a nonthreatening nurturing activity, a sustaining relationship, and a pleasing outcome. A

plant in a clear plastic cup shows its roots as well as its shoots—
a marvelous metaphor for things happening below the surface.

Hand Games

Preadolescents and even some teenagers enjoy thumb-wrestling,
hand-clap games, and making shadow puppets. These nonverbal
activities are highly interactive and require a degree of concen-
tration and new learning. Some informative texts on hand games
include:

- Jacobs, F. (1996). *Fun with hand shadows*. Dover.
- Achath, S. (1996). *Fun with hand shadows: Step-by-step instructions for more than 70 shadows from cud-chewing cows and dancing
  elephants to Margaret Thatcher and Michael Jackson.* NTC/Con-
  temporary.
- Bernstein, S. (1994). *Hand Clap! Miss Mary Mack and 42 other
  handclapping games for kids.* Adams.
- Brown, M. (1985) *Hand rhymes.* Dutton.
- Mariotti, M. (1989). *Hanimations.* Kane/Miller.
- Mayer, A. (1983). *Official book of thumb wrestling game board
  book.* Workman.

Hobbies

Kids with hobbies have richer lives. They have something to
absorb them besides school, family, and psychic pain. No-talk
therapy can be just the forum to research and develop a hobby,
which then goes with the child wherever he goes. Helping a
child or adolescent get started on a hobby also provides an auto-
matic topic for conversation and a shared interest. Some of the
more obvious and accessible hobbies include:

- Crafts: weaving, quilting, knitting, jewelry, collages, ori-
  gami, pillows

- Collecting: stamps, coins, sports cards, bottlecaps, Beanie Babies, comics
- Building: models, woodworking
- Magic: magic tricks, card tricks
- Period dollhouses, model railroads
- Ham radio

Homework

Sometimes kids come to therapy so anxious and burdened by the homework they have to do that it is difficult for them even to have fun. While it is not advisable to become a full-time tutor, it can be both nurturing and informative to help them over a homework hump from time to time. Getting the essay outline out of the way opens up time to do something else and positions the therapist as an ally in school struggles.

Jokes and Riddles

Some of us will sink to almost any depth to get a smile or at least a wince of pleasure out of a kid. No wisecrack, pun, bathroom joke, or inane riddle is beneath us. For the over-forty and joke-impaired therapists who can't remember any good ones, there are many joke books out there. Here's a resource guide to get you started:

- *Dr. Richard Gardner's Jokes and Riddles* (Audiotape—Creative Therapeutics 1-800-544-6162)
- Kilgarriff, M. (1991). *1,000 more jokes for kids*. Ballentine.
- Kilgarriff, M. (1990). *1,000 knock-knock jokes for kids*. Ballentine.
- Rovin, L. (1990). *500 hilarious jokes for kids*. New American Library.
- *Stupid jokes for kids*. (1991). Ballantine.
- Lederer, R. (1996). *Puns and games: Jokes, riddles, daffynitions, tairy fales, rhymes and more wordplay for kids*. Chicago Review Press.

Journals

Some older children and adolescents are able to communicate with therapists through a journal that goes back and forth. The therapist asks and answers questions, reacts to material in the journal, and always encourages more writing, in poetry or prose.

Knots

Learning how to tie a variety of knots isn't just for sailors and Boy Scouts. It offers simple skill development and can be turned into a not-so-subtle metaphor for the multitude of knots to untie in life.

Magic Tricks

In his explanation for why he uses magic tricks in therapy, Shapiro (1994) writes:

> Magic tricks have been popular with many therapists as a way to engage and interest the child. Therapists often see themselves as "magicians" so why not use a few tricks? Sometimes therapists will use magic to engage a child in therapy or to motivate him. A therapist may demonstrate a trick to a child, and then show him the "secret" behind the trick as a reward at a later date . . . good magic involves a wide variety of cognitive and social skills, including:
>
> - Telling a story (patter)
> - Mastery (having learned something that other people don't know and then demonstrating it)
> - Getting someone's attention in a positive way
> - Making a "connection" with the audience
> - Persistence (in practicing the trick)
> - Self-control (in showing the trick)
> - Problem-solving (if the trick goes wrong or the audience doesn't react the way you want them to) (pp. 69–70)

Magic is also a wonderful vehicle for no-talk therapy when the therapist is learning a trick for the first time, too. This levels the playing field, and no one has a knowledge advantage. Magic is also a convenient metaphor for *kids'* lives—they posses powers people can't see or understand. Simple magic tricks can be purchased at toy and novelty stores; some easy books on the topic include:

- Baron, H. (1995). *Magic for beginners.* Prima.
- *The party magician kit* (1993). Watermill Press.
- Baille, M. (1992). *Magic fun.* Little, Brown.
- Gordon. L. (1996). *52 cool tricks for kids.* Chronicle Books.
- Morlock, D. (1995). *Magic tricks for kids.* Morlock Associates.
- Lewis. S. (1990). *Shari Lewis presents 101 magic tricks for kids to do.* Random House.
- Cassidy, J. (1989). *The Klutz book of magic.* Klutz Press.

Maps

No-talk kids are sometimes astonishingly disoriented. Mapmaking—of their room, their street, their community, where they fit into the state,—can lead to some interesting discussions about belonging and how a child sees her place in the world.

Marbles

Marbles provide a turn-taking, rule-exploring, side-by-side sorting, conversation-limited, rollicking good time. There are dozens of marbles games; packages of marbles come with instructions.

Masks

Mask-making is a successful strategy for therapists wanting to pursue the idea that we hide behind masks of different personas—and that the no-talk facade is but one of many ways a child can reveal herself.

The Me Box

The point of the Me Box is to help the child focus on positive aspects of her life and identity. To make a Me Box, the no-talk kid decorates a shoebox with photos and cutouts that reflect her particular interests and affections. Then, every day for a month, she tries to write a sentence that reflects something positive in her life from that day or to throw in a symbol of something fun or good that happened (a good grade, a movie stub). When the box is full, it can serve as a handy reminder of better times. (This is not an exercise for kids whose unwillingness to talk stems primarily from depression and suicidality; they won't be able to fill the box until they feel better.)

The Miracle Question

When no-talk kids are particularly stuck and demoralized, this solution-focused approach can sometimes be helpful. Adapted from the work of Steve de Shazer (1988), the miracle question can be worded something like: "If a miracle happened in the middle of the night and your life no longer sucked, what would be different, and what would you be *doing* differently?" This exercise can get kids to envision a time when things will be better and to suggest some ways they might be managing their lives more effectively right now.

Movies

Sometimes sending a kid to the movies is a great intervention. (This strategy has the happy side effect of leading *us* to see more films ourselves.) Movies offer a wonderful chronicle of development throughout the ages, in a format most children and adolescents enjoy. Without necessarily leading to a lot of deep conversation, making movie recommendations to kids allows them consider a multitude of relevant issues. Therapists can also watch parts of movies with kids right in the office or make suggestions for the home VCR. Kids can also recommend movies for us to see. Besides browsing for the right match of movie and child, a couple of books provide handy references:

- Goldstein, R. (1980). *The screen image of youth: Movies about children and adolescents.* Scarecrow Press.
- Hesley, J. & Hesley, J. (1998). *Rent two films and let's talk in the morning: Using popular movies in psychotherapy.* Wiley.

Music

Music can be a universal connector. Make music, listen to music, drum, sing, dance, hum, play kazoos together. Some no-talk kids are brilliant blowing on a kazoo to show their feeings "musically"; others can use a guitar or keyboard to express their emotions. Kids can also convey their reactions through dance and movement.

Periscopes

Periscopes can be purchased or, better yet, built. Like therapy itself, they enable us to see things we might not otherwise know about.

Photographs

Some no-talk kids speak volumes with a camera of their own. Give them a chance to *show* you what they focus on. Do they shoot from 50 feet away or close up, people or objects? Do they have favorite themes or click at random? Make a book of their photos, adding captions if they are willing. Alternatively, have kids bring in their family photos and make a photo-essay of their lives.

Puppets and Plays

Puppet shows are a staple of traditional play therapy, and puppets offer a marvelous alternative mode of communication to no-talk kids of all ages. It helps to have a basket of irresistible puppets conveniently situated, so that a "bored" child or adolescent will happen upon it. Even no-talk kids will speak through puppets, and even young adolescents may be interested in conversing puppet to puppet. Puppet work can be used to build toward a show, act out an event, or simply converse.

Puzzles

Work on an ongoing jigsaw puzzle can provide the context for a more relaxed therapy with a no-talk adolescent. Other kinds of puzzles and Tangrams for younger kids also have many no-talk ingredients: collaboration, problem-solving, pleasure, a product.

Rainy Day Letters

Two types of rainy day letters help establish healing in no-talk therapy: letters and cards we write to the kids, and letters the kids write to themselves. Early in treatment, it is often helpful to write kids to say hello, summarize what happened in therapy, and indicate pleasure in the thought of a future meeting. It can be more powerful than a therapy session for a kid to realize you are thinking of him during the week. The most unexpected kids will keep letters you write them.

The rainy day letter they write themselves is designed to provide comfort to them at a later time. At a time when the child or adolescent has had a good day or week, this is recorded, in the most hopeful tone possible, and sealed. Later, when things are not going so well, the no-talk kid can open the letter as reminder of better times.

Kids can also benefit from writing other types of letters: to people who have abused them, people they miss, the president, the tooth fairy, or any other person who has particular meaning for them at a particular time in therapy. The letter can be a safe way to make contact with the past. It doesn't necessarily have to be mailed.

Regression

Sometimes it can be therapeutic to play a game or do an activity that seems way below a child's chronological age. Kids are often comforted by doing something that contains absolutely no challenge, something that may represent for them a time and place when their lives weren't this hard. Good regressive ideas include, for example, fingerpaints, sand, mud, and water play, simple board games like Candyland and Chutes and Ladders, card games like "War" and "Bullshit," play food, and doctor's kits.

Relaxation

We often underestimate the stress and chaos of kids' lives (though taking a trip to a middle school during the time between classes should increase our respect for them). Sometimes the quiet in our offices is the most peaceful and relaxing hour in the week for these children and adolescents; we can sit quietly with them and be most helpful if we *do* nothing at all. We can help them become more calm and centered using guided imagery, hypnosis, and standard relaxation techniques. All kids should have a few solid stress-management strategies, but this is especially important for no-talk kids. The wonder of most relaxation strategies is that the therapist does the talking as part of the technique, or silence reigns, thus sidestepping, for a time, the question of dialogue.

Role Reversal

Many no-talk kids have difficulty seeing things as others do. They hold rigidly to their position and refuse to see the problem with it. At times, a role reversal can be very helpful. Switch seats, and you be the no-talk kid. He gets to be the therapist and ask you anything he likes. He gets to figure out how to be helpful (while seeing his own behavior enacted before him). He can take notes, and he even has the option of consulting with one of your colleagues—about *you*. This exercise is best with kids who are engaged with you already and have a sense of humor. It needs to be practiced with some degree of levity, or it can turn into a struggle for both of you.

Secret Codes

For kids who won't talk, a secret code has a certain appeal. This activity also builds the private therapy relationship. The codes can be different letters of the alphabet, designs, morse code, or even semaphore signals (which sailors use). Invisible ink can also be a big enticement to make initial contact. For some kids, posing as secret agents and pretending to operate under a veil of secrecy are activities that are more likely to establish contact. Cryptography and code-breaking are already the stuff of therapy on other levels.

Silence

Occasionally, a no-talk kid will lead such a noisy, chaotic life that the only place of peace and quiet she knows is the therapist's office. Formalize the silence. Offer children and adolescents a few minutes at the beginning and end of sessions to feel that amiable quiet that comes from being together and not saying a word.

Soap

While not the most obvious therapy activity, soap flakes can be whipped up and put in cookie cutter molds to make "gift soaps" or used on realistic winter paintings. Again, the point of this activity is process (making something together) and product (having artwork or gifts to take home). Young adolescent girls are especially partial to gift soaps. Additionally, a sink of soap-suds and a few water toys can be a relaxing and mutually satisfying way to connect with a younger no-talk kid.

Social Action

Sometimes, angry and alienated adolescents need a constructive way to channel their concerns. No-talk therapy can connect them to larger causes, with a lot of positive benefits. For example, kids can become members of environmental groups (e.g., Earth First, Sierra Club), animal protection groups (e.g., Humane Society, World Wildlife Federation), social justice groups (e.g., Amnesty International, Habitat for Humanity), or groups working for many other excellent causes. As participants, they will receive mail, have an expanding identity, develop interests, and find a new peer group. The therapist and child joining together provides an immediate context for therapy and for what is important *to them*.

Storywriting and Storytelling

The "story" in all its forms and levels is, of course, the stuff of many kinds of therapy. In fact, one of the frustrations of no-talk work is the degree to which a story must be inferred and extrapolated. Child therapists have developed a great number of storytelling and storywriting interventions aimed at uncovering the information kids can't talk about directly. A few of these techniques include:

The Autobiography

A life book, a time line, a multimedia presentation, a dictated saga, an illustrated account, any way of recapping a life up to the present moment. Essential for kids in foster care or placement, helpful for many to assist them in remembering where they've been and who they are.

The Rewrite

Kids who are carrying around stories of traumatization also harbor frightening fantasies of retribution. When the story is out, we can help them "rewrite" new outcomes, featuring them as the powerful figures.

Modern Fairy Tales

Read or write down a favorite classical fairy tale or fable as the child recalls it. Then, together, recreate it for modern times, with a new outcome and a new moral.

Metaphoric and Hypnotic Stories

Sometimes we can tell stories to no-talk kids that have a subtext we want them to hear. Without talking directly about a problem, we can speak to their undefended imaginations. They don't have to speak to us to get going in therapy, as long as we do the storytelling. We can make up stories, describe "other patients we have treated," or use stories taken from some of the pros, including:

- Gardner, R. (1986). *The psychotherapeutic techniques of Richard A. Gardner.* Creative Therapeutics.
- Mills, J.C., & Crowley, R. (1986). *Therapeutic metaphors for children and the child within.* Brunner/Mazel.
- Brett, D. (1988). *Annie stories.* Workman.
- Mellon, N. (1998). *The Art of storytelling.* Element.

Shared Stories

These kinds of stories afford a kind of dialogue between therapist and child or adolescent, with each building upon the ideas of the other, beginning at "Once upon a time," and concluding with "The end." Each participant adds a few lines of plot or dialogue, leaving off for the next one, letting the story unfold as a shared vision.

Projective Stories

Kids tell stories to accompany pictures illustrating scenes, conflicts, or ambiguous activities. This exercise brings up the inner experiences of children without the threatening aspects inherent in actually talking about themselves. Projective storytelling cards and games are available from Childswork Childsplay.

Scrapbooks

A story doesn't have to be written with words. It can also contain memorabilia from places and people, cutouts from magazines and objects of interest. No-talk kids can make interesting scrapbooks of their lives or a period of their lives.

"Storybook Weaver"

A program that offers ideas and scenery for illustrated stories written on the computer.

Poetry

For literary therapists, kids' poetry writing can be very freeing and revealing. A detailed discussion of how to engage kids in writing poetry can be found in:

• Koch, K. (1970). *Wishes, lies and dreams*. Harper.

Telephones

Younger children may prefer conversing about things on a play phone or different extensions in the same office. Older kids may even do better having occasional sessions phoned in from the comfort of their own homes. They are much more accustomed to the medium of the telephone than the medium of therapy.

Telephones can also be an interesting method of breaking the sense of isolation that no-talk kids often experience. For example, kids who have moved can be helped to call friends from their old neighborhood or school, old babysitters, or relatives they miss. Kids who are fearful of using the phone can also call from the safety of the therapist's office to make play dates or converse with someone they would like to befriend.

Telephones are also a resource. Call the reference librarian, the hospital, a lawyer, or someone else who might be able to answer a pressing question that you might have. Kids can learn that resources are all around and in this way become less isolated.

Tents and Pillows

Frightened kids like cozy, safe places. From a little pup tent or under a nest of pillows, no-talk kids may even become quite conversational.

Time Capsules

Together with the no-talk kid collect symbols of who she is right now—pictures, vital statistics, wrappers from her favorite foods, collages of interests, etc.—and assemble the items in a box or tin, sealed tightly. Decide when you'll open it before burying or stashing it in a safe place. This activity reveals something of how the child sees herself at this point in time; it also suggests to her that she will be interesting to you in the future.

Videotapes

Videotapes have become a staple of child and family therapy, and they can also work with some no-talk kids. They can be used to record accomplishments and products such as sculptures, artwork, plants, puppet shows, and successful negotiations. At the end of treatment, they can be used as a record of a time together or to teach other children with similar problems. Older kids can make documentaries or show the therapist what is important to them outside the therapy room. Kids who are living apart from one or both parents can send videotapes of their accomplishments to them. Families of no-talk kids can go home and review work they have done in sessions.

The Wise Old Person

This hypnotic exercise is adapted for children and teenagers from the work of Yvonne Dolan (1991). The Wise Old Person strategy has a couple of fine implications: Kids *are* going to grow older and wiser, and they possess within them the knowledge to get unstuck. Additionally, they don't have to tell you what they have thought of—this, too, they can keep to themselves. Dolan directs her patients to:

> Imagine that you have grown to be a healthy, wise old woman and you are looking back on this period of your life. What do you think that this wonderful, older, wiser you would suggest to you to help you get through this current phase of your life? What would she tell you to remember? What would she suggest that would be most helpful in helping you heal from the past? What would she say to comfort you? And does she have any advice about how therapy could be most useful and helpful? (p. 36)

Kids can think this through, with eyes closed, or write their older, wiser selves a letter and then assume the role of the older, wiser person and write back. Over time, they can also "check in" with their wise old self whenever they get stuck. The wise old person becomes a handy problem-solving and self-soothing resource.

Writing Letters

Kids can write famous people and usually hear back from them. Help kids write the President, a favorite TV star, a band, or a local representative asking for information or pictures. This activity can make kids feel powerful indeed, even before they get a reply.

Yo-Yos

Yo-yos are a perennial favorite of no-talk kids, and provide a fine symbolic end to this book addressing the ups and downs of no-talk therapy. Learning how to yo-yo isn't hard, though some of the fine points take a while to master. These titles will help you get started:

- Sayco, L. (1998). *The ultimate yo-yo book*. Grosset & Dunlap.
- Klutz Press. (1987). *The Klutz yo-yo book*. Klutz Press.

References

Achenbach, T., & Howell, C. (1993). Are American children's problems getting worse? A thirteen year comparison. *Journal of the American Academy of Child and Adolescent Psychiatry, 32*(6), 1145–1154.

Amaya-Jackson, L., & March, J. (1995). Post-traumatic stress disorder. In J. March (Ed.), *Anxiety disorders in children and adolescents* (pp. 276–300). New York: Guilford.

American Psychological Association (1993). *Summary report of the American Psychological Association's Commission on violence and youth: Vol 1. Violence and youth: Psychology's response.* Washington, DC: American Psychological Association.

American Psychological Association (1996). *Violence and the family.* Washington, DC: American Psychological Association.

Anthony, E. J., & Cohler, B. J. (Eds.). (1987). *The invulnerable child.* New York: Guilford.

Armbruster, P., & Kazdin, A. (1994). Attrition in child psychotherapy. In T. H. Ollendick & R. J. Prinz (Eds.), *Advances in clinical child psychology* (Vol. 16, pp. 81–108). New York: Plenum.

Axline, V. (1947). *Play therapy.* Boston, MA: Houghton Mifflin.

Bandura, A. (1977). Self-efficacy: Toward a unifying theory of behavior change. *Psychological Review, 84*, 191–215.

Barragar Dunne, P. (1992). *The narrative therapist and the arts.* Los Angeles: Possibilities Press.

Beck, A. (1976). *Cognitive therapy and the emotional disorders.* New York: International Universities Press.

Berndt, T., & Savin-Williams, R. (1993). Peer relationships and friendships. In P. Tolan & B. Cohler (Eds.), *Handbook of clinical research and practice with adolescents* (pp. 203–220). New York: Wiley.

Berry, C. (1989). *When helping you is hurting me.* New York: HarperCollins.

Bettelheim, B., & Rosenfeld, A. A. (1992). *The art of the obvious: Developing insight for psychotherapy and everyday life.* New York: Knopf.

Bowlby, J. (1988). *A secure base: Parent child attachment and healthy human development.* New York: BasicBooks.

Brems, C. (1993). *A comprehensive guide to child psychotherapy.* Needham Heights, MA: Allyn & Bacon.

Bronfenbrenner, U., & Weiss, H. (1983). Beyond policies without people: An ecological perspective on child and family policy. In E. Zigler, S. Kagan, & E. Klugman (Eds.), *Children, families and government* (p. 398). New York: Cambridge University Press.

Brooks, R. (1991). *The self-esteem teacher.* Circle Pines, MN: American Guidance Service.

Brooks, R. (1994). Children at risk: Fostering resilience and hope. *Journal of Orthopsychiatry, 64*, 545–553.

Browne, J. (1979). *These days.* Los Angeles, CA: Warner-Tamerlane.

Byrne, N. (1997). Family therapy: Terminable and interminable. *Clinical Child Psychology and Psychiatry, 2*(1), 167–175.

Cederborg, A. (1997). Young children's participation in family therapy. *American Journal of Family Therapy, 25*(1), 28–38.

Chethik, M. (1989). *Techniques of child therapy.* New York: Guilford.

Children's Defense Fund. (1998). Where America stands. *CDF Reports, 19*(2), 2.

Cohler, B. J. (1987). Adversity, resiliency and the study of lives. In J. Anthony & B. Cohler (Eds.), *The invulnerable child* (pp. 363–424). New York: Guilford.

Cole, P., Michel, M., & O'Donnell, L. (1994). The development of emotion regulation and dysregulation: A clinical perspective. In N. Fox (Ed.), *Monographs of the society for research on child development* (Vol. 59, pp. 73–100).

Cowan, P. (1988). Developmental psychopathology: A nine-cell map of the territory. In E. Nannis & P. Cowan (Eds.), *Developmental psychopathology and its treatment* (pp. 5–30). San Francisco: Jossey-Bass.

Davis, L., & Tolan, P. (1993). Alternative and preventive interventions. In P. Tolan & B. Cohler (Eds.), *Clinical research and practice with adolescents* (pp. 427–452). New York: Wiley.

de Shazer, S. (1988). *Clues: Investigating solutions in brief therapy.* New York: Norton.

Deci, E. L., & Chandler, C. (1986). The importance of motivation for the future of the LD field. *Journal of Learning Disabilities, 19*, 587–594.

Dewald, P. (1980). Forced termination of psychotherapy: The annually recurrent trauma. *Psychiatric Opinion, January*, 13–15.

Dodge, K. (1989). Problems in social relationships. In E. Mash & R. Barkley (Eds.), *Treatment of childhood disorders* (pp. 222–246). New York: Guilford.

Dolan, Y. (1991). *Resolving sexual abuse.* New York: Norton.

Donaldson, S., & Westerman, M. (1986). Development of children's understanding of ambivalence and causal theories of emotion. *Developmental Psychology, 26*, 655–662.

Donner, R. (1997). *Program Uplift: WrapAround services to adolescents.* Paper presented at the Parsons/SUNY Empire State Fall Institute, Albany, NY.

Dozier, M., Cue, K., & Barnett, L. (1994). Clinicians as caregivers: Role of attachment organization in treatment. *Journal of Consulting and Clinical Psychology, 62*, 793–800.

Dryfoos, J. (1990). *Adolescents at risk.* New York: Oxford.

Dyregrov, A., & Mitchell, J. T. (1992). Work with traumatized children: Psychological effects and coping strategies. *Journal of Traumatic Stress, 5*, 5–17.

Elkind, D. (1985). *The hurried child.* Reading, MA: Addison-Wesley.

Epston, D., & White, M. (1992). *Experience, contradiction, narrative, and imagination: Selected papers of David Epston & Michael White 1989–1991.* Adelaide, Australia: Dulwich Centre Publications.

Epston, D., White, M., & "Ben". (1995). Consulting your consultants: A means to the co-construction of alternative knowledges. In S. Friedman (Ed.), *The reflecting team in action: Collaborative practice in family therapy* (pp. 277–313). New York: Guilford.

Erickson, J. (1986). Non-formal education in organizations for American youth. *Children Today, January-February*, 17–23.

Erikson, E. (1963). *Childhood and society.* New York: Norton.

Fenwick, E., & Smith, T. (1996). *Adolescence.* New York: DK Publishing.

Figley, C. R. (Ed.). (1995). *Compassion fatigue.* New York: Brunner/Mazel.

Freedman, S. (1993). *Upon this rock: The miracles of a black church.* New York: HarperCollins.

Freeman, J., Epston, D., & Lobovits, D. (1997). *Playful approaches to serious problems.* New York: Norton.

Freud, A. (1968). Indications and contraindications for child analysis. *Psychoanalytic Study of the Child, 23*, 37–46.

Freud, S. (1909). Phobia in a five year old boy, *Collected Papers* (Vol. 3, pp. 149–195). New York: BasicBooks.

Freud, S. (1930/1961). *Civilization and its discontents.* New York: Norton.

Garbarino, J. (1995). *Raising children in a socially toxic environment.* San Francisco: Jossey-Bass.

Gardner, R. (1975). *Psychotherapeutic approaches to the resistant child.* New York: Jason Aronson.

Garmezy, N. (1983). Stressors of childhood. In N. Garmezy & M. Rutter (Eds.), *Stress, coping and development in children* (pp. 43–84). New York: McGraw-Hill.

Gillman, R. D. (1991). Termination in psychotherapy with children and adolescents. In A. Schmikler (Ed.), *Saying goodbye: A casebook of termination in child and adolescent analysis and therapy* (pp. 339–354). Hillsdale, NJ: The Analytic Press.

Greene, R. (1998). *The explosive child.* New York: HarperCollins.

Greenberg, L., & Safran, J. (1987). *Emotion in psychotherapy.* New York: Guilford.

Grosch, W. N., & Olsen, D. C. (1994). *When helping starts to hurt: A new look at burn-out among psychotherapists.* New York: Norton.

Guerra, N. (1993). Cognitive development. In P. Tolan & B. Cohler (Eds.), *Handbook of clinical research and practice with adolescents* (pp. 45–62). New York: Wiley.

Hallowell, E. (1996). *When you worry about the child you love.* New York: Simon & Schuster.

Hanks, M. (1981). Youth voluntary associations and political socialization. *Social Forces, 11,* 211–223.

Hanks, M., & Eckland, B. (1978). Adult voluntary associations and adolescent socialization. *Sociological Quarterly, 19*(3), 481–490.

Harter, S. (1993). Causes and consequences of low self-esteem in children and adolescents. In R. F. Baumeister (Ed.), *Self-esteem: The puzzle of low self-regard* (pp. 87–111). New York: Plenum.

Harter, S., & Whitesell, N. (1989). Developmental changes in children's understanding of single, multiple and blended emotion concepts. In C. Saarni & P. Harris (Eds.), *Children's understanding of emotion* (pp. 81–116). New York: Cambridge University Press.

Healy, J. (1990). *Endangered minds.* New York: Simon & Schuster.

Herman, J. (1992). *Trauma and recovery.* New York: BasicBooks.

Hewlett, S. (1991). *When the bough breaks: The cost of neglecting our children.* New York: Harper.

Institute for Social Research. (September, 1986). The "quality time" myth. *International time management and productivity newsletter,* pp. 1–2.

James, B. (1989). *Treating traumatized children.* Lexington, MA: Lexington Books.

James, B. (1994). *Handbook for treatment of attachment-trauma problems in children.* Lexington, MA: Lexington Books.

Jones, M. (1924). A laboratory study of fear: The case of Peter. *Pedagogical Seminary, 31,* 308–315.

Kagan, J. (1984). *The nature of the child.* New York: BasicBooks.

Kagan, R. (1996). *Turmoil to turning points: Building hope for children in crisis placements.* New York: Norton.

Karr-Morse, R., & Wiley, M. (1998). *Ghosts from the nursery: Tracing the roots of violence.* New York: Atlantic Monthly Press.

Kazdin, A. (1988). *Child psychotherapy: Developing and identifying effective treatments.* New York: Pergamon.

Kazdin, A. (1991). Effectiveness of psychotherapy with children and adolescents. *Journal of Consulting and Clinical Psychology, 59,* 785–789.

Kazdin, A. (1996). Dropping out of child psychotherapy: Issues for research and implications for practice. *Clinical Child Psychology and Psychiatry, 1*(1), 133–156.

Kazdin, A., Mazurick, J., & Siegel, T. (1994). Treatment outcome among children with externalizing disorder who terminate prematurely versus those who complete. *Journal of the American Academy of Child and Adolescent Psychiatry,* 549–557.

Kendall, P., Lerner, R., & Craighead, W. (1984). Human development and intervention in child psychopathology. *Child Development, 55*, 71–82.

Lyon, E. (1993). Hospital staff reactions to accounts by survivors of childhood abuse. *American Journal of Orthopsychiatry, 63*, 410–416.

Males, M. (1996). *The scapegoat generation: America's war on adolescents.* Monroe, ME: Common Courage.

Murphy, L. B. (1987). Further reflections on resilience. In E. J. Anthony & B. J. Cohler (Eds.), *The invulnerable child* (pp. 84–105). New York: Guilford.

Novick, J., Benson, R., & Rembar, J. (1981). Patterns of termination in an outpatient clinic for children and adolescents. *Journal of the American Academy for Child Psychiatry, 20*, 834–844.

Olson, K. (1993). *A narrative study of resilience in physically abused people.* Unpublished doctoral dissertation. Antioch New England Graduate School, Keene, NH.

Otto, L. (1975). Extracurricular activities in the educational attainment process. *Rural Sociology, 40*, 162–176.

Parker, J., & Asher, S. (1987). Peer relations and later personal adjustment: Are low-accepted children at risk? *Psychological Bulletin, 102*, 357–389.

Pearce, J. W., & Pezzot-Pearce, T. D. (1997). *Psychotherapy of abused and neglected children.* New York: Guilford.

Piaget, J. (1954). *The construction of reality in the child.* New York: BasicBooks.

Pipher, M. (1994). *Reviving Ophelia.* New York: Putnam.

Plunkett, J. (1984). Parent's treatment expectations and attrition from a child psychiatric service. *Journal of Clinical Psychology, 40*, 372–377.

Repucci, N. D. (1987). Prevention and ecology: Teen-age pregnancy, child sexual abuse and organized youth sports. *American Journal of Community Psychology, 15*, 1–22.

Rogers, C. (1942). *Counseling and psychotherapy.* Boston, MA: Houghton Mifflin.

Ryan, W. (1971). *Blaming the victim.* New York: Vintage.

Safran, J. (1990). Towards a refinement of cognitive therapy in light of interpersonal theory. *Clinical Psychology Review, 10*, 87–121.

Segrave, J. U., & Chu, D. B. (1978). Athletics and juvenile delinquency. *Review of Sport and Leisure, 3*, 1–24.

Select Committee on Children, Youth and Families (1989). *U.S. children and their families: Current conditions and recent trends.* Washington, DC: U.S. House of Representatives.

Selekman, M. (1997). *Solution-focused therapy with children: Harnessing family strengths for systemic change.* New York: Guilford.

Shapiro, L. (1993). *The book of psychotherapeutic games.* King of Prussia, PA: Center for Applied Psychology, Inc.

Shapiro, L. (1994). *Tricks of the trade.* King of Prussia: Center for Applied Psychology.

Shirk, S., & Russell, R. (1996). *Change processes in child psychotherapy.* New York: Guilford.

Shirk, S., & Saiz, C. (1992). Clinical, empirical and developmental perspectives on the therapeutic relationship in child psychotherapy. *Development and Psychopathology, 4,* 713–728.

Simons, J., Finlay, B., & Yang, A. (1991). *The adolescent and young adult fact book.* Washington, DC: Children's Defense Fund.

Smith, W., & Rossman, R. (1986). Developmental changes in trait and situational denial under stress in childhood. *Journal of Child Psychology and Psychiatry, 27,* 227–235.

Steele, B. F. (1986). Notes on the lasting effects of early abuse throughout the lifecycle. *Child Abuse and Neglect, 10,* 283–291.

Stern, D. (1985). *The interpersonal world of the infant.* New York: BasicBooks.

Straus, M. (1994). *Violence in the lives of adolescents.* New York: Norton.

Strupp, H. (1986). The nonspecific hypothesis of therapeutic effectiveness: A current assessment. *American Journal of Orthopsychiatry, 56,* 513–520.

Strupp, H. (1989). Psychotherapy: Can the practitioner learn from the researcher. *American Psychologist, 44,* 717–724.

Stuart, S., Pilkonis, P., Heape, C., Smith, K., & Fisher, B. (1991). *The patient-therapist match in psychotherapy: Effects of secure attachment and personality style.* Paper presented at the Meetings of the North American Chapter of the Society for Psychotherapy Research, Lyons, France.

Szasz, T. (1974). *The myth of mental illness.* New York: Harper & Row.

United States Department of Education. (1987). *What works: Research about teaching and learning, 2nd ed.* Washington, DC: U.S. Department of Education.

Valentin, C. (1984). *The mentor and the dream: Facilitators of psychosocial competence in inner city adolescents.* Unpublished Doctoral Dissertation. Dissertation Abstracts International.

Weisz, J., Weiss, B., Alicke, M., & Klotz, M. (1987). Effectiveness of psychotherapy with children and adolescents. *Journal of Consulting and Clinical Psychology, 55,* 542–549.

Werner, E. (1988). Individual differences, universal needs: A 30–year study of resilient high-risk infants. *Birth to Three, 8,* 1–5.

Werner, E. (1989). High-risk children in young adulthood: A longitudinal study-birth to 32 years. *American Journal of Orthopsychiatry, 59,* 72–81.

White, M., & Epston, D. (1990). *Narrative means to therapeutic ends.* New York: Norton.

Winnicott, D.W. (1971). *Playing and reality.* New York: Basic Books.

Youth and America's Future. (1988). *The forgotten half: Pathways to success for America's youth and young families.* Washington, DC: William T. Grant Foundation Commission on Work, Family and Citizenship.

Zimrim, H. (1986). A profile of survival. *Child Abuse and Neglect, 10,* 339–349

Index